The
Sibling
Estrangement
Journal

Other books by Fern Schumer Chapman

Non-Fiction

Brothers, Sisters, Strangers: Sibling Estrangement and the Road to Reconciliation

Memoir

Motherland: A Mother/Daughter Journey to Reclaim the Past

Young Adult Historical Fiction

Is It Night or Day?

Young Adult Non-Fiction

Stumbling on History: An Art Project Compels a Small German Town to Face Its Past

Like Finding My Twin: How an Eighth-Grade Class Reunited Two Holocaust Refugees

Three Stars in the Night Sky: A Refugee Family's Odyssey of Separation and Reunion

Children's Picture Books

Happy Harper Thursdays: A Grandmother's Love for Her Granddaughter during the Coronavirus

The Return of Happy Harper Thursdays: The Guiding Light of a Grandmother's Love

For more information, please visit: www.fernschumerchapman.com

Praise for Fern Schumer Chapman's
first book about sibling estrangement—
Brothers, Sisters, Strangers:
Sibling Estrangement and the Road to Reconciliation

For more information, please visit: fernschumerchapman.com

"Deeply moving . . . The author's vulnerability turns what could have been a clinical look at family dysfunction into a sensitive, compassionate narrative. Even cynics will find hope in this story of redemption."
—*Publishers Weekly*

"A terrific, compassionate, much-needed book about broken family relationships and the path to healing."
—Dr. Wendy Mogel, *New York Times* bestselling author of *The Blessing of a Skinned Knee*

"A primer in mending familial fences blended with an affecting memoir."
—*Kirkus Reviews*

"Fern Schumer Chapman is a superb writer. In this stunning family memoir, she fearlessly probes the forty-year estrangement from her brother and chronicles their uneasy road to reconciliation. Along the way, she deftly weaves in pertinent social science research, capturing the voices and insights of hundreds of people suffering from sibling alienation. *Brothers, Sisters, Strangers* deserves to be read and discussed for years to come."
—James B. Lieber, Pulitzer Prize-nominated author of *Friendly Takeover*

"No better book presents the subject of sibling estrangement in such a far-reaching, personal, and practical way. A must-read!"
—Ali-John Chaudhary, psychotherapist and administrator of the Facebook page,
   Sibling Estrangement—Sharing, Coping, Connecting

The Sibling Estrangement Journal

A guided exploration of your experience
through writing

Fern Schumer Chapman

Author of *Brothers, Sisters, Strangers: Sibling Estrangement and the Road to Reconciliation*

 GUSSIE ROSE PRESS
Published by Gussie Rose Press

ISBN: 979-8-9872597-0-2 (paperback)

Welcome to *The Sibling Estrangement Journal!*

You have picked up this workbook because you, or someone you care about, struggles with a broken sibling relationship. You may be completely cut off from a loved one. You may have chosen to terminate the relationship to protect yourself. You may have simply grown apart. You may be grieving because a brother or sister decided, against your wishes, to remove you from his or her life.

In any case, no matter how the rift occurred, most estranged siblings mourn the loss of the relationship—whether it was one they treasured, or one they merely hoped for. Many feel shame and guilt about the failure of the relationship.

For the better part of 40 years, I had almost no relationship with my only sibling, an older brother. I can't recall a specific fight or incident that led to our estrangement. We just didn't have much to say to each other, and, in time, we said nothing at all.

In the early years of our cutoff, I tried to sustain a connection with him. I reached out many times, but he was unresponsive. Finally, I quit trying. I couldn't *force* him to have a relationship with me.

Eventually I barely knew who my brother was: where he worked, what he loved, how he spent his days. I hadn't seen him in so many years that I wasn't sure I would recognize him if I saw him on the street, and I scrupulously avoided any place where I might see him. Even that possibility was too painful.

And yet—though I recognized the distance between us, the degree to which our values didn't coincide, the tangible reasons we had grown up to be vastly different people—I simply could not understand the actual estrangement. I ruminated endlessly on this incomprehensible situation: an utter contradiction of the very nature of family, an aggressive rejection of how almost all living creatures fundamentally organize themselves.

Questions nagged at me: *Am I alone in my suffering? Do other people live in a constant state of mourning the living? What does this failure say about me? How should I explain to my children that they'll never know their cousins on my side of the family? Can I prevent other family members from being caught up in the split? How should I portray this cutoff to friends and family when I didn't understand it myself? If I couldn't trust my only sibling to want a relationship with me, whom could I trust? Given my loss, will I ever be able to find a sense of balance and well-being?*

Sibling estrangement often carries profound hurt and a deep stigma. As I wrote in my book, *Brothers, Sisters, Strangers: Sibling Estrangement and the Road to Reconciliation,* I realized early on the disturbing nature of how others perceive a rupture in a sibling relationship.

Few want to admit to this level of family dysfunction, even though the experience is quite common. One of the rare studies that quantifies this phenomenon came from Michigan's Oakland University. Its survey showed that one out of three people struggle with siblings, describing their relationship as apathetic or openly hostile.

For some, estrangement raises elemental doubts about oneself. For others, it is a necessary choice to avoid more hurt. Either way, few friends or family members unacquainted with the estrangement understand the experience and the depth of the guilt, shame, or pain. And even fewer want to talk about it.

Support groups exist for the estranged, but many who endure this trauma are reluctant to join as the scars of sibling estrangement can be severe. And, of course, not everyone can afford private therapy to address the hurt and its fallout. Consequently, many suffer in silence, isolated twice: not only from our sibling, but also from social support against the loss.

This writing journal offers a private, emotional outlet to understand and process the grief of sibling estrangement. Putting feelings into words brings relief. Here are a few comments from those who have used expressive writing as therapy:

— *It feels therapeutic to tell my story again.*
— *It helped me to think more deeply about the nature of my sibling estrangement instead of just feeling bad and anxious about it. It was challenging to answer the questions, but it ultimately helped me to move forward.*
— *Once I recorded on the page some of my feelings about sibling estrangement, I didn't carry around the same sadness and weight.*

The work of Dr. James Pennebaker, a pioneer in writing therapy who teaches in the psychology department at the University of Texas at Austin, confirms the value of emotional or expressive writing as a form of narrative therapy. In a landmark research project, he identified potential health benefits from the practice of writing from the heart for 20 minutes a day. Pennebaker's research has been replicated and validated hundreds of times, particularly for those who suffer with PTSD.

Dr. Pennebaker recommends that you write non-stop for 20 minutes a day to make sense of your emotions and to construct meaning from your experiences. You may want to take weeks or months to complete this writing workbook. The pace you set is entirely up to you.

The 20 chapters and subsequent questions will help you write from the heart. Here, you can identify privately, within your own experiences and their significance *to you*, the signs of a toxic sibling relationship. You can explore the rumination and thought patterns that often result from a cutoff. And you can help the estranged—yourself and others—find a way to endure the loss of a living family member.

Here, you'll answer probing questions that help you connect the dots in your own behavior which play out in your sibling relationship. By answering the questions in this journal—regardless of whether you are the shunner (estranger) or the shunned (estrangee)—you will develop new ways of thinking about your estrangement that will help you move forward. You will reach powerful realizations, gaining insight through your own writing and discovering your own resilience and truth.

Social psychologist Karl Weick is known for his wise saying: "How do I know what I think until I see what I say?" His point is that people don't have clear points of view until they have the occasion and opportunity to express them.

Here, you'll learn what you think by seeing what you write. Be honest; be brave. It won't always feel good, but you *will* feel better.

Empowering Principles for Estranged Siblings

Few resources exist for estranged siblings. Therefore, psychotherapist Ali-John Chaudhary has created a private Facebook group, *Sibling Estrangement—Sharing, Coping, Connecting*, that serves as an important online support group for estrangers and estrangees.

https://www.facebook.com/groups/688926101896419

This Facebook page has identified guiding principles for those estranged from siblings in its mission statement. Re-read these useful and empowering principles when needed.

- I have a right to be myself and no one can take that away from me.

- I am so much more than what my sibling thinks of me.

- I can't change the past, but I can define how much contact with my sibling, if any, is right for me.

- I have the choice to stop replaying the tape when my thoughts, feelings, and responses get me down.

- I will seek to put my safety and well-being as my number one priority in my sibling relationship.

- I will work to recognize what I control and don't control in my sibling dynamic.

- I have value and self-worth, even on days when I may feel down.

- I have the right to belong and be part of a community or group that supports me.

- The most important relationship you will ever have is the one with yourself. Nurture it.

Reprinted with permission from psychotherapist Ali-John Chaudhary, administrator of *Sibling Estrangement—Sharing, Coping, Connecting*.

Table of Contents

Understanding Sibling Estrangement

Chapter 1
The Pain of Ambiguous Family Estrangement
A variety of tactics can limit closeness.

KEY POINTS

- Usually, there are two parties in an estrangement.
- Siblings use a variety of tactics to control how close they are to a brother or sister.
- Some siblings alternate between breaking and resuming contact, cycling through estrangement and reconciliation.

When a 63-year-old Friend learned that I was conducting a survey on sibling estrangement for my book, he emailed me to see if he qualified.

Twenty-five years had passed, he explained, since his older brother and he had argued over a family business matter. Ever since, they've had little to do with each other. They are cordial when they see each other at family events, but that's it; they remain ultimately distant:

"I hear from my brother once in a while—when someone dies or when our mother is ill in the hospital," he said. "Once a year or so, he'll leave me a message on my birthday or for some other reason. But I haven't really talked to him or his wife in years. Is this estrangement?"

The answer is yes. Kristina Scharp, an assistant professor and director of the Family Communication and Relationships Lab at University of Washington, and one of the few researchers on the topic, has created a working definition of estrangement: "It is a process where at least one family member voluntarily and intentionally distances themselves from another family member because of an ongoing (perceived) negative relationship."

The word "estrangement" is rooted in two Latin words: *extranear* means "to treat as a stranger," and *estraneus* means "not belonging to the family." In sibling estrangement, the two concepts come together.

Defining Those Involved in Estrangement

A sibling may choose to physically or emotionally distance from a brother or sister to reduce conflict, anxiety, or tension in the relationship. While estrangement may spread to other family members, there are usually two parties in an estrangement:

- **Estrangee:** This is the person who has been cut off by a sibling. He or she has not chosen to dissolve the relationship.

- **Estranger:** This is the person who cuts off from a sibling. In doing so, a brother or sister may withdraw emotionally, maintain social and/or physical distance, and stop contact without ever explaining his or her reasons.

Over the years, some people switch between being an estrangee or estranger. No matter which party is which, however, both are estranged. In the case of siblings, they lack trust and emotional intimacy; often, their differences extend to having divergent values and lifestyles. The estrangement indicates that they can't find a way to re-establish their relationship.

Various Types of Estrangement

As my friend realized, some sibling relationships may become ambiguous before sliding into estrangement. A sibling may have no idea why a brother or sister has become distant or terminated the relationship. They wonder: *Have I done something wrong? Is there something bad about me? How can I fix this?*

When the relationship limps along, a sibling may find a variety of ways to control the "thermostat" of its intimacy. Estrangements often fall into the following categories:

- **Emotional estrangement:** A sibling might deny family members emotional information—important details, even basic facts—about his or her feelings or personal life. Siblings who have infrequent, uncomfortable, obligatory contact at weddings, funerals, or holidays are experiencing a limited relationship or emotional estrangement. In this situation, siblings often feel anxious when they know they're about to have contact. When together, they may be pleasant and polite, avoiding contentious topics. In time, however, such a relationship often degenerates into hostility, passive-aggressive behavior, and open conflict. Siblings who are increasingly emotionally estranged typically spend less and less time in each other's presence, and the relationship sometimes dwindles away to nothing.

- **Physical estrangement:** Siblings may drastically reduce contact or completely stop seeing each other. The estrangement may happen after an insulting comment or a missed holiday—even just a raised eyebrow—but a physical estrangement actually may be the culmination of decades of unaddressed slights and irritations. Deeper issues and resentments can build up over time; often it's these factors, not the perceived "last straw," that form the true roots of a cutoff. In extreme circumstances—such as abuse, neglect, incest, alcoholism, addiction, or criminal behavior—therapists may recommend that a sibling end contact with a family member. Even in the absence of such drastically intolerable circumstances, a sibling who feels chronically hurt, belittled, or betrayed may choose this option for self-protection, bringing an end to the toxic behavior.

- **Geographic estrangement:** To avoid unresolvable feelings of rage and resentment, a sibling may simply relocate far away from the family. This is a convenient way to maintain distance without requiring much justification or explanation. While today's intensely connected society poses challenges to a total lack of contact, "out of sight, out of mind" still holds true.

Testing Different Types of Estrangement

Many siblings alternate between breaking and resuming contact, cycling through various types of estrangements and reconciliations, resulting in a chronic state of chaos. They may push limits, testing whether they can (or want to) tolerate a complete breakdown. Years may go by as the parties try to find a mutually acceptable level of involvement. In other cases, especially when one party is the more aggrieved, the siblings just let time and distance do the work of enforcing an estrangement.

However, maintaining distance can be more difficult than establishing the cutoff in the first place. Families who might support ending an abusive marriage may pressure the estranged to repair rifts with siblings, even when the relationship is abusive. And every time holidays roll around or a relative gets married or dies, the estranged are forced to reevaluate and sometimes redefine the cutoff.

Every relationship carries its own unique nuances, its own ups and downs. When estrangement slips and slides along a spectrum bounded by "getting along OK" and "dead to me," the sibling who wants a better connection must make every effort to attain internal clarity. It's crucial to think carefully and realistically when analyzing the potential costs, benefits, and possibilities of mending an estrangement.

References

Agllias, K. (2017). *Family Estrangement: A Matter of Perspective*, Routledge, London and New York.

When did you feel safe and loved with your sibling? When did you not? Do you think about or miss your estranged sibling? What events or moments bring your sibling to mind?

Describe your estrangement from your sibling, including what you feel is most important about this experience. (*For example: your prior relationship, your feelings about the break, what caused the break, what effect the estrangement has had on parenting or family.*) What are some of the defining moments from your adult relationship with your sibling?

How do you connect with your sibling right now? What is left unsaid between the two of you? What would you say if you could say anything, and why haven't you said it?

_____

_____

_____

_____

_____

_____

_____

_____

_____

_____

_____

_____

_____

_____

_____

_____

Chapter 2
Eight Things People Need to Understand About Sibling Estrangement

7. Yes, you can mourn for a living person.

KEY POINTS

- Some feel judged, embarrassed, and humiliated that they can't sustain a relationship with a sibling.
- One common misperception is that no one else struggles to maintain a relationship with a sibling.
- Some estranged siblings wonder, "Is there something wrong with me because I can't get along with my brother or sister?"

For years, I never told anyone how my estrangement from my only brother had created a gaping hole in my life. My secrecy arose from one simple but powerful reason: I feared I would be judged.

Most people project onto others their notions of what a family should look like—a pretty picture that echoes throughout our culture. From Shakespeare to sitcoms, family bonds are idealized. I found it humiliating that I couldn't negotiate some sort of relationship with my own brother. How could I explain the experience to someone else when I didn't understand it myself?

Making matters worse, I didn't want to admit that my family experienced this level of dysfunction, and others who are estranged often feel the same way; they suffer in silence, rarely discussing the experience. The stigma, alienation, and silence surrounding this painful topic create fertile ground for misperceptions about sibling estrangement.

Here are eight:

1. I'm the only one who is estranged from my sibling.

Those who are estranged often believe that nobody else has a rough or chaotic relationship with a sibling. Psychotherapist Ali John Chaudhary, who specializes in this topic and has created several resources for estranged siblings, says that many who are cut off from relatives are black sheep—family members who are treated differently, marginalized, or excluded, and typically blamed for whatever goes wrong in the family. "It helps to recognize that others struggle, too," Chaudhary says. "In fact, studies show that the number is as high as one in three sibling relationships that are strained or estranged."

2. There must be something wrong with me if I can't get along with my sibling.

Many factors can sour a sibling relationship: a lack of shared interests, power struggles, personality disorders, just plain bad chemistry. No matter how serious or trivial the roots, sibling rejection ripples into many areas of life and identity. It can damage your sense of who you are, how you see your friendships and other social relationships, your self-esteem, your ability to trust, even your physical well-being. One of Chaudhary's mantras is, "I am so much more than what my sibling thinks of me."

3. Family always comes first.

Family does not come first when it's toxic. Instead, prioritizing boundaries and a sense of security is vital. You aren't obligated to do everything for the sake of the family if you run the risk of eroding yourself. Chaudhary emphasizes that no one has the right to take you away from you.

4. I'm totally responsible for my sibling relationship.

Those who are deeply empathic often hold this belief. Yet a sibling may be concerned only with his or her own issues, insecurities, and attempts to dominate and gain power, especially if he or she is narcissistic. Assuming full responsibility often leads to enabling.

5. Things will be different the next time we get together.

There's a label for this misperception: "Euphoric recall" is a state in which people remember the past through "rose-colored glasses," exaggerating positive experiences while suppressing the negative side. This feeds the notion that things will somehow improve, even though that's unlikely. (More on euphoric recall in Chapter 10.) Chaudhary says it's important to create a plan when you expect to see an estranged sibling. Doing something different could improve the encounter; optimism alone isn't enough.

6. I need to get along with my sibling for my parents' sake.

Even if you must spend time with your sibling, beware of neglecting your own needs. If you do, you run the risk of becoming a people-pleaser. (More on people-pleasing in Chapter 7.) There may be times when you choose to buy peace by accommodating. However, doing so repeatedly can make you an enabler. Failing to set boundaries—for your parents' or anyone else's sake—gives your brother or sister power over you.

7. I can't be mourning a living person.

Impossible as it seems, we often grieve for the living. A sibling's conscious choice to excise you from their life can be more devastating than mourning the dead. Death is final; the door has closed on that relationship. With estrangement, there's often an enduring hope that things might change. "Complicated grief" is marked by intense yearning, longing, or emotional pain; frequent, preoccupying thoughts and memories of the absent person, and an inability to accept the loss. I call it mourning the living.

8. Only family can give me a true sense of belonging.

Creating close, healthy relationships with others outside the family nurtures a sense of belonging. "Voluntary kin can serve as excellent sources of support and fulfill the roles we associate with family," says Kristina Scharp, an assistant professor and director of the Family Communication and Relationships Lab at the University of Washington. "Many people have a difficult time separating the idea of family from biology and law. Yet there is nothing inherent about biology or the law that guarantees a happy or satisfying sibling relationship."

What are the feelings you have experienced or are experiencing due to sibling estrangement? Do you feel hurt and rejected or liberated? What feelings in your body do you notice when you think about your sibling?

_____

_____

_____

_____

_____

_____

_____

_____

_____

_____

_____

_____

_____

_____

_____

_____

Describe how your siblings see you. Are they accurate? Identify some of the common ways you both perceive the estrangement. Try writing about the cutoff from the perspective of your estranged sibling. (*Use "I" when writing from his or her perspective.*)

_____

_____

_____

_____

_____

_____

_____

_____

_____

_____

_____

_____

_____

_____

_____

Which of the eight points in this chapter surprise you? Why? Describe your family's expectations of you and your siblings. Can you be your authentic self with your siblings and your family in general?

_____

_____

_____

_____

_____

_____

_____

_____

_____

_____

_____

_____

_____

_____

_____

_____

Chapter 3
Five Moments When Siblings Are Most at Risk of Estrangement
2. The introduction of a new in-law.

KEY POINTS

- Estrangement often occurs when a sibling's life changes, and he or she must redefine his or her role in the family.
- To steer clear of a sibling cutoff, being mindful of the risk factors for estrangement can help.
- Siblings renegotiate their relationship over time.

Certain moments are especially vulnerable for the sibling relationship, as brothers and sisters must renegotiate how they interact with one another over the course of a lifetime. In fact, estrangement often occurs when a sibling's life circumstances change, and he or she must redefine his or her role in the family.

Here are some of the perilous turning points in sibling relationships:

Adolescence

A teenage sibling, individuating and creating his or her own identity, leaves home for college or a job. He or she may challenge parental authority, changing the established sibling relationships and dynamics in the family.

When my older brother left for college, he wanted to leave behind the dysfunction and difficult relationships in our family. While he and I were never particularly close, we did have a sibling connection. However, at this moment, he chose to leave the past behind him, and our relationship became a casualty of his desire to abandon the problems of the family.

Marriage

A new in-law joins the family and may want to control how much time the couple will spend with parents and siblings. The new in-law may have values and beliefs that differ from those of the original family, although such issues aren't essential to cause strife.

At one possible extreme, a sibling or child marries someone who turns out to be a narcissist. One reader wrote to me about how her new daughter-in-law removed her son from the family: "It started slowly and in time the spouse has increased with more and more control, brainwashing, and gaslighting on our son. Our narcissistic daughter-in-law seems to have a calculated plan. She has completely changed our son and cut him off from the family. Nothing we do in his and my granddaughters' lives seems to change this." (More on narcissism in Chapter 5.)

Birth of a Baby

As a sibling focuses on his or her new family, some family members may feel abandoned or betrayed. Often, sibling rivalry continues into adulthood; siblings may even compete with each other through their children.

At its worst, an estrangement occurs, and aunts and uncles may be heartbroken if they don't have the opportunity to develop a relationship with their nieces and nephews. Estranged siblings, when denied the role of aunt or uncle, also may find that their children suffer from not having the opportunity to know their cousins.

Indeed, children often are caught in the crossfire of sibling estrangement, with damage extending through generations. When her nieces were young, one woman said, she enjoyed a close relationship with them. But when her sister cut her off, she lost relations with the entire family. Being deprived of the relationship with her nieces, she said, has been more devastating than the estrangement from her sister.

Divorce and Marital Problems

The emotional and possible financial responsibilities of helping a divorcing family member—or one whose marriage is in trouble—may overwhelm one sibling, creating disagreements over how to handle the situation or resentment at an unevenly shared burden.

In an especially painful twist, one woman revealed the truth when she learned that her brother-in-law was cheating on her sister. But the sister, far from confronting her husband, essentially "killed the messenger" by instead terminating her relationship with the sister who had shared the disturbing news.

Parental Illness, Death, or Inheritance

Siblings may stage a last-ditch competition for power, love, and family loyalty. Difficult conflicts arise over who will make health care arrangements and payments for an elderly parent, who will pay for long-term care, and who will inherit treasured family possessions.

Fights over money may become especially vicious as a parent approaches the last stage of life. Divisive topics, such as health-care decisions and caregiving needs, may reignite old conflicts. Often, caregiving falls disproportionately to one sibling. Caring for parents as they decline is a relentless, painful vigil that may cause unprecedented strain and stress.

A parent's death may add to the pressure, rather than relieve it. Unresolved estate issues can entangle estranged siblings, and, in some cases, siblings who have had years of separation suddenly must interact again.

In addition to these perilous turning points, there are many risk factors for sibling estrangement, which include:

- Family trauma
- Parental Favoritism
- Sibling Jealousy
- Poor Communication Skills
- Family Values, Judgments, and Choices

- Political differences
- Alcoholism, addiction, and other mental health issues
- Money
- Narcissistic families and siblings

The next chapter will explore these risk factors in depth. Those who hope to steer clear of a sibling cutoff should be mindful of the risk factors for a cutoff, as well as the perilous moments when a sibling relationship is most vulnerable.

Describe a time when you redefined your role in your family. What consequences did it have on your sibling(s)?

_____

_____

_____

_____

_____

_____

_____

_____

_____

_____

_____

_____

_____

_____

_____

Which "turning points" in your relationship with your sibling(s) altered your connection with your brother or sister? How did things change? Do you treat yourself compassionately when you remember these moments, or are you filled with self-blame?

When you "renegotiated" your relationship with your sibling, did you discuss the changes or simply alter your behavior? Looking back, what do you wish you could do over with your sibling?

_____

_____

_____

_____

_____

_____

_____

_____

_____

_____

_____

_____

_____

_____

_____

Chapter 4
Ten Things That Can Drive Adult Siblings Apart

Trauma, jealousy, money, and more.

KEY POINTS

- Sibling estrangement is grossly under investigated, but researchers have identified risk factors within families.
- A feeling of not 'belonging' to family, and a lack of attention or actual presence by parents can contribute to poor sibling relations.
- Narcissism, money, poor communication, parental favoritism, sibling jealousy, and political differences are all risk factors for estrangement.

In 2014, when a possibility of reconciliation with my estranged brother surfaced, I was determined to do everything possible to reestablish a connection—and never let it go.

I sent myself on a quest to understand the complexities of sibling estrangement. I soon realized that the topic is grossly unacknowledged and under-investigated. Nonetheless, I was surprised to learn that social science research has identified certain risk factors that increase the chances of a sibling cutoff.

Here are 10 risk factors for sibling estrangement:

1. Family Trauma

Children raised in chaotic, abusive, or neglectful families, run the greatest risk of estrangement, as many are living with parents who have an authoritarian parenting style. These parents are "demanding, highly critical, and shaming," according to Kylie Agllias, author of *Family Estrangement: A Matter of Perspective*. They often use scapegoating, favoritism, and name-calling when relating to their children.

Long-term disconnection in childhood is a frequent precursor to estrangement. "This disconnection may be characterized by a lack of early attachment experiences," writes Agllias. It involves "a feeling of not 'belonging' to family, and a distinct lack of attention or actual presence by the parent or parents."

Children tend to respond to turmoil with one of two behaviors: They may form a close bond based on their shared traumas, or, more often, they protect themselves by isolating from the family. Children who experience or witness trauma in early life may shut down, numbing themselves to their emotions, which eventually limits all of their relationships.

2. Parental Favoritism

Children are sensitive to parental favoritism, a factor leading to estrangement. Research by Karl Pillemer, a sociologist, gerontologist, and professor of human development at Cornell University, suggests that between two-thirds and three-quarters of mothers have a favorite child, and that children are keenly aware of a parent's partiality.

When a parent favors a child, that sibling may become more egocentric, which could lead to estrangement. The "golden child" places his or her needs above the family as well as its other members, explains psychotherapist Ali-John Chaudhary, who practices in Pembroke, Ontario. "That's where a sense of entitlement grows," he says, "and favored children become hostile towards those who have different needs than them. Parents need to teach that child that the family comes first, and individual needs come second."

3. Sibling Jealousy

Two personality types appear to be vulnerable to estrangement: those who are chronically angry and those who nurse grievances. The issues that divide siblings in adulthood, according to psychologists Joel Milgram, Professor Emeritus of Education at the University of Cincinnati, and the late Professor Helgola Ross, often stem from rivalries over achievement, looks, and intellect.

4. Poor Communication Skills

The roots of estrangement may be found in poor communication skills, often originating with parents. When parents are unable to express feelings and negotiate differences civilly, they don't model the necessary skills—listening, apologizing, cooling off—that show children how to resolve conflicts. As a result, small disagreements can escalate, sometimes exploding into nasty rifts. Adults with poor communication skills may handle stress or strife in a relationship by shutting down and cutting off.

5. Family Values, Judgments, and Choices

The sense that a sibling has rejected the family's core beliefs may spark estrangement. Those who challenge the family's values through sexual orientation, interracial marriage, religious conversion, political philosophies, unconventional career, or lifestyle choices may find themselves cast out.

Some families simply will not tolerate behaviors that are perceived as deviating from the family identity. "The 'family myth' is the presumption that every family member is compatible, possesses the same goals, and loves one another," explains psychologist Mark Sichel, director of the Addiction Recovery Unit at Hebrew Union College, New York. The author of *Healing from Family Rifts*, Sichel explains that families may use "we" statements coercively, to assert common values and discourage individual differences.

6. Political Differences

In today's charged political atmosphere, the smallest offense can shatter a sibling bond made brittle by partisanship. Shared beliefs are built on shared values, and some family foundations have collapsed around sociopolitical cracks. To mask or not to mask, to vax or not to vax, in-person or remote learning: These and other issues rooted in politics have created or deepened fissures in families and sibling relationships.

7. Alcoholism, Addiction, and Other Mental Health Issues

Some serious problems—such as mental illness, substance abuse, incest, and violence—may never even be mentioned, much less discussed, in a family setting. Yet they may lead to cutoffs. Agllias's research shows that mental illness and addiction (problems that are often related) aren't typically the sole cause of estrangements, though drugs and alcohol may fuel abuse and domestic violence. These mental health issues are indicators, and possibly causes, of broader family problems.

8. Money

Not surprisingly, issues of money and possessions often rupture sibling relations. *Why wasn't that loan repaid? Who's getting Grandma's jewelry? Why was that child promoted in the family business?* These and similar questions plague many families, often dividing siblings.

9 Inheritance and Elderly Care

Existing fights may turn vicious as a parent approaches the last stage of life. Divisive topics, such as health-care decisions and caregiving needs, may reignite old conflicts. When parental illness, death, or unresolved estate issues confront estranged siblings, things may worsen as they suddenly must interact again.

10. Narcissistic Families and Siblings

An exaggerated sense of self-importance and entitlement; arrogance and haughtiness; a tendency to monopolize conversations and belittle "inferiors," and a general failure to recognize the needs of others. All these characterize a narcissist.

Narcissistic parents often create a competitive environment where children are pitted against their siblings. The children may have experienced narcissistic triangulation, when a family member tried to control the flow, interpretation, and nuances of communication. Children reared in narcissistic homes rarely feel closely connected as adults, and when one sibling is narcissistic, the relationship is at great risk for estrangement. The next chapter will take a closer look at narcissism and sibling estrangement.

REFERENCES

Agllias, Kylie (2017) *Family Estrangement: A Matter of Perspective.* Routledge, London and New York

Describe the home and family dynamics in which you were raised (*peaceful, tumultuous, loving, abusive, disconnected, etc.*) Describe your relationship with your sibling prior to the estrangement. Write about specific memories that support your perceptions. What scenes from your childhood stand out in your mind?

Describe how your parents related to each other and how they related to each child in the family. What kind of communication skills were modeled in your family? Did you learn how to discuss and negotiate differences as they arose?

This chapter lists ten risk factors for estrangement. Identify which of the ten you have experienced and provide as many details as you can to support your selections.

_____

_____

_____

_____

_____

_____

_____

_____

_____

_____

_____

_____

_____

_____

_____

_____

Chapter 5
Is a Narcissistic Sibling the Reason for Your Estrangement?

Narcissism often is a factor that contributes to sibling estrangement.

KEY POINTS

- Narcissism often is rooted in the original family where children were pitted against each other.

- Parents may enable narcissistic siblings by excusing bad behavior and insisting that the family stay together at all costs.

- Ending the sibling relationship is sometimes the only way to stop the cruel and abusive behavior.

Many estranged siblings realize over time that a brother's or sister's narcissistic tendencies are the underlying cause of their toxic relationship.

That's what happened to Karen Martin, 65, a Californian who is estranged from her older brothers. All three are narcissistic, she says; she has a limited relationship with one, none at all with the others. She describes her sibling complexities:

> It's difficult to sustain sibling relationships with three brothers who are narcissistic. They always get upset over trivial things. Underlying every conversation is envy and competition. No matter what subject comes up, they have to be right.

> All of them are very bright, and each needs to be better than the other, and each needs extreme approbation. Sometimes it shows up in small ways. I'd ask one brother, "What's the weather?" He would answer by telling me about meteorological isotopes. He had to show that he's not inferior. All

of them monopolize conversations so they are the center of attention. Life is a game they need to win.

They completely lack empathy. Around others, I feel loved and admired, but around them, I feel unacknowledged. There is no exchange of ideas or validating conversation. I don't get anything out of these relationships.

They were envious of me because I was the only girl and the youngest, and they felt my parents favored me. But they don't realize that, as an adult, I've really worked on maintaining a fulfilling relationship with my parents. They never did.

None of the brothers talk to each other now, and I don't talk to two of them. All are toxic.

When I don't hear from any of them, I'm relieved because I don't worry about when the next earthquake will hit. Also, I really don't like the person I become when I'm with the one brother I still talk to. I'm a strong, assertive woman, but around him, I become frightened and tentative, and I succumb to his demands. Sometimes, when he calls and I see his name on my cell phone, I begin to shake. Around him, I lose myself quickly.

Karen's description identifies many characteristics of narcissistic people:

- Changing the rules; "moving the goal posts" to benefit themselves
- Lacking empathy; never recognizing the needs of others
- Consistently being entitled and arrogant
- Altering reality to their benefit: defending or rationalizing self-serving behavior; deflecting blame; lying to exaggerate their own achievements
- Gaslighting to persuade others that they're mistaken in their perceptions
- "Shape-shifting" to misrepresent personal traits or an entire identity at will
- Manipulating others to their advantage
- Engaging in cruel behaviors to obtain advantage or just to inflict misery
- Triangulating; pitting people against each other
- Belittling, invalidating, and ignoring those they consider inferior
- Monopolizing conversations; demanding constant attention
- Disrespecting boundaries; feeling entitled that they needn't comply with others' wishes.
- Betraying confidence
- Launching "campaigns" against others: making themselves look perfect and their sibling look like the "crazy" one
- Competing so relentlessly that the jealousy and rivalry between adult siblings leads the non-narcissistic sibling to give up on spending time together

- Avoiding responsibility; blaming others; apologizing rarely (if ever)
- Taking advantage of others with cunning style and charm

Siblings Who Experience Narcissistic Abuse

Siblings like Karen Martin have had to study narcissism to understand their family dynamics. Many are fluent in the psychological language of narcissism. They speak of the following:

- "Gray rocking"—a way to interact with a narcissistic person, by being boring and unemotional like a gray rock
- "Hoovering"—when narcissistic persons suck their victims back into the relationship
- "Flying monkeys"—other people who act on behalf of a narcissistic person, usually for abusive purposes

Many in narcissistic families complain that as children they were pitted against their siblings. Often, a sibling's narcissistic characteristics and injuries were evident when siblings were young. Typically, narcissistic siblings keep score and feel compelled to outplay a sibling. They often triangulate in the family, playing two against one. Children reared in narcissistic homes rarely feel connected to one another as adults.

As adults, narcissistic siblings believe they're entitled to more of a parent's attention or money, although they're not interested in helping to care for parents. Adult siblings of narcissistic individuals often find themselves in a confusing, twisted reality when a toxic sibling abuses the victim, who, predictably, reacts with anger. The toxic person then responds by accusing the victim of being abusive. It is difficult to sustain any kind of relationship when these patterns are repeated. This places the relationship at great risk for estrangement.

Parents often enable narcissistic siblings by excusing bad behavior and requiring a sibling to be nice to his/her narcissistic brother or sister. The parents may insist that family comes first, even when the relationships are abusive. In some cases, siblings must break away from the entire family to protect themselves from a narcissistic sibling's damaging behavior.

Those who have experienced narcissistic abuse often struggle with the following:

- confusion
- anxiety
- self-blame
- self-doubt
- helplessness
- rumination
- grief

How to Handle a Narcissistic Sibling

Narcissistic people rarely make changes. Even in therapy, they may lack the ability to reflect on and recognize their role in a dysfunctional relationship.

Therefore, siblings who are abused by a narcissistic brother or sister should protect themselves by setting solid boundaries. Determine what behaviors you'll tolerate, communicate your boundaries, and decide on a consequence. If your sibling violates that boundary, enforce the consequence.

If the relationship is violent or so toxic that you are chronically hurt, consider ending contact. Another possibility is a limited relationship in which you effectively manage your exposure and maintain a superficial relationship with the toxic sibling.

Dr. Sherrie Campbell, author of *Your Pocket Therapist: Quick Hacks for Dealing with Toxic People While Empowering Yourself*, advocates ending the abusive person's ability to continue the behavior: "It's unhealthy for us to keep taking the abuse. We need to take care of ourselves."

REFERENCES

Torgersen, S. Epidemiology. Oldham JM, Skodol AE, Bender DS. *The American Psychiatric Publishing Textbook of Personality Disorders*. Washington, DC: American Psychiatric Publishing; 2005. 129-141.

Behary, W. T. (2013). *Disarming the Narcissist: Surviving and Thriving with the Self-Absorbed*. New Harbinger Publications.

During your childhood, in what ways were you pitted against your sibling? Can you give specific examples? What do you feel were the consequences of that kind of child-rearing?

What experiences have you had with narcissistic family members? Can you identify some of the behavior patterns of a toxic sibling? Describe how narcissism affected your ability to sustain these relationships.

In your opinion, what are the best strategies to deal with a narcissistic sibling? Describe and assess what strategies have worked best for you when you have had to interact or maintain a relationship with a family member with narcissistic tendencies.

Chapter 6
The Shame and Isolation of Sibling Estrangement
Others typically see a cutoff as a personal failure

KEY POINTS

- Regardless of the reasons for the cutoff, estranged siblings are caught in a swirl of judgments and doubts.
- A survey of estranged family members found that 68 percent feel judged and stigmatized by the cutoff.
- The estranged feel judged by a culture that expects family cohesion, and they often view the cutoff as a personal failing.

Tell someone "I'm divorced," and they probably won't blink an eye; indeed, they may be eager to share their own divorce saga. Tell someone "I don't get along with my mother," and chances are good they'll roll their eyes empathetically.

But if you say, "I have no relationship with my brother," people don't relate as easily. They get uncomfortable, arch their eyebrows, and probably wonder

— *What's wrong with her?*

— *Is this a good candidate for friendship?*

— *If she can't maintain a relationship with her own brother, is she capable of sustaining any relationship?*

While writing my first book on sibling estrangement, I interviewed a woman who said that people can't believe the stories she tells them about her family. Nor do they accept her decision to opt out. "Some say I should make things work no matter what because it's family," she explained. "One person even told me that it must be my fault since they've all cut me off."

Estrangement casts suspicion on everyone involved. Whether estrangement was a choice or the relationship simply faded away, estranged siblings are caught in a swirl of judgments and doubts. The sibling who ends contact—the shunner or estranger—may be haunted by the daunting question: *How could I be so heartless as to cut off my own sibling?* Meanwhile, the shunned or the estrangee may be plagued by the corresponding question: *What's wrong with me that my sibling doesn't want anything to do with me?*

Both shunned and shunner find themselves on high alert to others' perceptions of their possible failings. People often don't offer their explicit thoughts about an estrangement, but an eye-roll, averted gaze, or awkward silence betrays their discomfort. Those nonverbal signals often give the estranged the feeling that they have something shameful to hide. Many of the estranged I interviewed expressed frustration that a wide array of disturbing topics, from divorce to abuse, are openly discussed—yet sibling estrangement remains steeped in shame.

An important collaborative study by *Stand Alone*, a British organization that offers support services to estranged family members, and the University of Cambridge's Centre for Family Research sheds light on the stigma of estrangement. Analysis of 807 members of the *Stand Alone* community who completed the study's survey showed that 54 percent agreed with the statement that "estrangement or family breakdown is common in our family." Among adults estranged from one or more family members, 68 percent believed that a stigma accompanies family estrangement. Many respondents cited the fear of judgment and assumptions of fault or blame as a frequent source of shame.

Rejecting the Family Order

The idea of the close, loving extended family is a social construct that isn't necessarily representative of most families, yet it is reinforced everywhere. Throughout the culture, from opera to sitcom, brothers and sisters are assumed and urged not just to maintain, but also to prioritize, above all else, their families. "Blood is thicker than water!" and "Love thy family!" and "You can't choose your family!" and—yes, even—"There's no place like home."

Many people find the very idea of family estrangement so threatening that they can't confront, much less discuss, a family model that doesn't match their expectations. Few who haven't experienced estrangement understand the profound hurt, and even fewer want to talk about it.

Yet, whenever I tell people I've written a book about sibling estrangement, they sit up a little straighter and lean in, as if I've tapped into something. Even those who haven't experienced this loss likely know someone who has, and they welcome insights. One woman told me she suspects that the hidden pervasiveness and shame of estrangement resemble those behind the "Me Too" movement. So does the increased risk of low self-esteem that comes with hiding the problem.

Avoiding the Topic of Estrangement

Lacking an empathetic community or cultural support, some rejected siblings cope by evasion. They may dodge even casual questions about their family, redirecting the conversation in hopes of avoiding social disapproval. Some will go so far as to lie about their family.

Denial as a coping strategy can be difficult to sustain, especially in a small town. One woman whose military family lives in rural Arkansas says she doesn't tell anyone in town about her family estrangements. However, at her children's sporting events, where large extended families gather to cheer on young players, she can't hide her alienation. In the stands, she sits—conspicuously and uncomfortably—alone.

To the estranger or the estrangee, what's most shattering is their common question: *What does this say about me as a person?* Shunner and shunned alike carry the stigma of estrangement as their own personal failing, a character flaw, feeling invisible, meaningless, judged, and found wanting by a culture that celebrates and expects family cohesion.

In what ways have you been judged or stigmatized by sibling estrangement? How did these judgments make you feel?

_____

_____

_____

_____

_____

_____

_____

_____

_____

_____

_____

_____

_____

_____

_____

Do you explain the estrangement to your family and friends? If so, what do you say about the relationship? What stories are you afraid to tell your friends about your sibling estrangement? Why?

Describe a specific experience when you have felt shame and isolated because of your sibling estrangement? What is the story of your shame that's tied to sibling estrangement? Why do you think you have felt so alone?

The Ripple Effect of Sibling Estrangement

Chapter 7
How Estrangement Defines Other Relationships and Friendships

A family estrangement is traumatic, and it changes how an individual interacts.

KEY POINTS

- After an estrangement, many suffer from post-traumatic symptoms, such as emotional flashbacks, hyper-vigilance, and low self-esteem.

- Some say that a cutoff hurts their ability to trust anyone. They think: "If I can't trust my family, who can I trust?"

- Longing to replace the family they've lost, the estranged often resort to trauma responses, such as people-pleasing, fawning, or self-denial.

Estrangement is never just an isolated incident. Its trauma spreads both deep and wide, potentially creating a psychological landmine that fundamentally affects every other emotional connection.

Even when it's essential to end an abusive relationship, estrangers as well as estrangees may suffer a variety of long-term post-traumatic symptoms, according to a 2014 study by Kylie Agllias, a foremost expert on estrangement and author of *Family Estrangement: A Matter of Perspective*. These symptoms include:

- Flashbacks
- Hyper-vigilance
- High levels of shame and embarrassment
- Anxiety
- Hypersensitivity

- A form of survivor's guilt, questioning whether they should have done more to maintain the relationship
- Avoidance of anything related to or echoing the estrangement
- Poor self-esteem

Many estrangers view a cutoff as a matter of survival: the only avenue to health, happiness, and personal growth. Nonetheless, they may experience an intense need to recreate a sense of belonging, identity, and safety through non-family associations.

Yet the estranged may sabotage their own efforts by replicating the same traumatizing patterns. A sibling who can't individuate may become mired in dysfunctional childhood models, risking the repetition of destructive patterns in adult relationships.

Here's how one woman who was bullied by her two brothers described a disastrous attempt at a relationship:

> My last attempt at opposite-sex friendship played out like a giant karmic gong show. Mr. Sort-of-Right had on-again-off-again estrangement with his two siblings. He was the same age as and had a similar character to my volatile eldest bro and the same birth order position as my self-centered little bro. I unwittingly stepped into his big sister's shoes (read: "golden child") when I befriended his ailing elderly father. Sort-of-Right and I began to argue RE: "defining our relationship" ("undefined" was fine with me). My literal last words after he took a deliberately hurtful "negativity and pity parties" cheap shot RE: my sibling estrangements: "You're exactly like my two idiot brothers—you act and speak without thinking, fling hurtful sh-t at me, and never apologize!"

The Long Reach of Early Sibling Relationships

Siblings set the model for future relationships, so a cutoff from a brother or sister, even when necessary, can be uniquely damaging. As our earliest companions, siblings ideally reinforce in one another many crucial social qualities—tolerance, generosity, loyalty—that eventually shape our liaisons with friends, colleagues, and lovers. As children, siblings typically spend more time together than with anyone else; when they're lucky, their loving bond outlasts friendships, marriages, and even parents.

The bond also can be disturbing. "Childhood perceptions, feelings, hurts and resentments from these original experiences with siblings often haunt our lives," explains Dr. Karen Gail Lewis, author of *Siblings: The Ghosts of Childhood That Haunt Your Love and Work* and a counseling psychologist in Maryland who organizes guided retreats for siblings. Whether or not people are aware of these old feelings, she explains, they bring them into current situations, distorting how they react to siblings and others today. "We often engage in what is called sibling transference," she continues, "when adults transfer onto other important adults in their lives feelings they had about their siblings when they were little."

Inability to Trust

A failed sibling relationship can compromise the ability to trust and, consequently, to truly connect with others, whether romantically or merely as friends. Even those who choose to walk away from a destructive sibling wonder: "If I couldn't trust my own brother or sister, who can I trust?"

Many estranged siblings experience a "generalized reduction in trust," Agllias says, "which may affect their capacity to engage fully or openly in new relationships."

These comments from the survey I conducted for my first book on sibling estrangement reveal how estrangement shatters the capacity for trust:

— *I am afraid to make friends because I don't trust people. It is hard to trust anyone.*

— *I find it difficult to make friends. I have always been afraid of making long-term committed relationships with men because of my estrangement from my two older brothers. I don't want to repeat the horror of my early life.*

— *When a friend distances themselves from me for good reason (a crisis where they need to be alone), I get triggered and panicked. I feel like I am being taken for granted like my family did.*

Those who are cut off from family, Agllias explains, may impose on themselves a heavy pressure not to repeat the past. The uncertainty, self-doubt, and self-repression of this constant effort hardly constitute a winning relationship strategy.

People-pleasing as a Trauma Response

In their yearning to replace the family they've lost, some of the estranged seek reassurance and comfort in relationships that backfire. Their efforts to "get along" may create an enmeshed dependence that compromises their self-agency. Always yielding to a partner's wishes or needs, they become "people-pleasers."

Far from "just being nice," fawning or people-pleasing—extreme efforts to appease others—are a trauma response. People-pleasers avoid conflict by changing their behavior, often to an unhealthy, self-denying degree.

Here are ways this trauma response shows itself:

- Struggling to be "seen" by others
- Feeling anger and guilt toward oneself
- Difficulty saying "no" to others
- Compromising one's own values
- Being taken advantage of by others
- Feeling responsible for others' reactions
- Inability to identify and/or enforce clear personal boundaries
- Feelings of stress or discomfort when called upon for an opinion
- Codependence in relationships

Consequently, some estranged family members rush into unsuccessful marriages with the first person who declares love for them. Ultimately, they discover that their partners are manipulative and exploitative, just like a toxic family member.

Clearly, sibling estrangement isn't just a broken family bond. It profoundly stamps the estranged family member, who brings the devastating experience and its resulting harm—poor self-esteem, inability to trust, suppression of emotion, etc.—into other relationships.

REFERENCES

Agllias, K. (2014) Report on the adult child's experience of estrangement from at least one parent. Unpublished report. University of Newcastle.

What meaning do you assign to your estrangement? (*In other words, what does your estrangement say about you? For example, do you feel unloved and unlovable because you have a limited relationship with your sibling? Do you feel you can't trust anyone because you can't trust your sibling? Do you feel nothing ever works out for you?*) Assess whether the meaning you have assigned to this experience is an accurate portrayal of who you are.

Can you identify how you have engaged in sibling transference? How does your estrangement with your sibling affect your relationships with your parents, partner, children, and friendships? Be specific.

_____

_____

_____

_____

_____

_____

_____

_____

_____

_____

_____

_____

_____

_____

Are you a people-pleaser? Do you respond with fight or flight? Can you give examples of when you responded with fight or flight or people-pleasing? Are you fearful of being authentic in your sibling relationship? If so, what do you think will happen?

Chapter 8
How Family Estrangement
Echoes Across Generations

"My son couldn't even recognize his uncle on a train."

KEY POINTS

- Long-standing cutoffs often may be modeled and replicated in families, generation after generation.

- When someone is shunned—even by a stranger, even only briefly—the same area of the brain that registers physical pain is activated.

- Young people crave the sense of belonging a functioning family provides and, without it, they may turn to dangerous alternatives.

A revealing story of how estrangement ripples through generations comes from Marjorie Watson, 64, of Bangor, Maine.

To her regret, Marjorie has little contact with several family members, while her husband hasn't spoken to his sister and brother-in-law in more than 16 years. She discovered how that affected her children recently, when her adult son sat down on a train next to an oddly familiar-looking man.

As Marjorie relates:

> Discreetly, he used his iPhone to take a photo of his seatmate. Then he sent the photo and this text to me: "Mom, is this Uncle Michael?" I looked at the picture and, even though I hadn't seen him in years, I was sure it was him. But my son didn't introduce himself. It made me sad that my son couldn't even recognize his uncle on a train.

In cases of abuse and violence, cutoffs can be necessary and protective. However, in other families long-standing estrangements may become an acceptable model of coping with stress, replicated generation after generation. In these families, when conflict arises, siblings may easily cut each other off, having seen their parents do just that with their own brothers or sisters.

Responding to the survey I conducted for my book, *Brothers, Sisters, Strangers: Sibling Estrangement and the Road to Reconciliation*, 65-year-old Helene Pendergast of London blamed her family history for the 50-year heartache of having no relationship with her only brother. "Those who come from well-adjusted, happy families are most fortunate," she says. "If those who are estranged were to track their family histories for two or three hundred years, I am sure they would find that brokenness stretching way back."

The Need to Belong

The distinguished psychologist Abraham Maslow identified the crucial need to belong in his "Hierarchy of Needs," a meticulously defined pyramid ranking fundamental human requirements. The need to belong—whether through family, friendship, shared interests, or sexual intimacy —places just after the body's basics: food and water, shelter and sleep, and physical safety. And, like these fundamentals, the human need to belong is lifelong.

Without a sense of belonging—this feeling of emotional safety and context—people come to fear that their very lives are at risk. Their ability to trust others dwindles; they become consumed by the challenge of surviving alone.

The family—that original constellation of relationships—is the primary, natural place of belonging; it provides the opportunity to develop deep, lifelong connections transcending the transient nature of human existence. Exclusion can cause pain that cuts deeper and lasts longer than a physical injury, according to psychologist Kipling D. Williams of Purdue University, who is known for his studies of ostracism.

When someone is shunned—even by a stranger, even only briefly—Williams found that he or she experiences a strong, harmful reaction, activating the same area of the brain that registers physical pain. The difference is that social injuries linger: In studying more than 5,000 people, Williams used a computer game to reveal how just two or three minutes of ostracism can produce ongoing negative feelings.

"Our studies indicate that the initial reaction to ostracism is pain," he explains, "which is similarly felt by all individuals regardless of personality or social/situational factors. Ostracism then instigates actions aimed at recovering thwarted needs of belonging, self-esteem, control, and meaningful existence."

Multi-generational Cutoffs and Consequences

The deep divisions of estrangement may produce serious family complications. Siblings who aren't speaking can't discuss important issues: *What kind of care does our ailing father need? Should we move Mom out of the family home? Is it time to sell the family business?*

As estrangement ripples through the family, important historical and health-related information spanning generations may be lost. No one may know, for example, that a great-grandparent suffered an illness now plaguing a descendant—or how the condition was successfully treated.

Countless posts in estrangement chat rooms, as well as responses to my survey, describe how cutoffs damage children, stepchildren, and grandchildren. These young family members feel like "lone stars" in the universe, lacking a stable place in a recognized constellation. Young people typically crave the sense of belonging that a functioning family provides. When those needs aren't satisfied, they search elsewhere, substituting unrelated people—surrogate grandparents, aunts, uncles, cousins—for their missing relatives.

That search carries its own risks, as some young people may turn to more ominous alternatives. "The gang has quite a bit to offer the very young," explains sociologist Zina McGee of Hampton University in Virginia, who is the author of *Silenced Voices: Readings in Violence and Victimization*. "There is that sense of acceptance, there is that sense of value that comes from being a member of that gang. [The young] gain their sense of self from that group."

A 2010 survey found that many gang-involved youth feel cut off from their families. The survey, sponsored by The Alfred P. Sloan Foundation and conducted by psychologists at the Emory Center for Myth and Ritual in American Life, asked adolescents about their family histories and if they knew stories about their ancestors. Those adolescents who had personal knowledge of their family history, this research demonstrated, had a greater sense of well-being. They tended to be higher achievers, and their families generally were more stable and functional.

Clearly, when estrangement echoes through generations, adults and children don't only lose family members who might play an important role in their lives. They also suffer the lingering pain and consequences of ostracism and isolation.

REFERENCES

Kip Williams, "Kip Williams Media Contact Overview," last edited January 29, 2020, Social Psychology Network, williams.socialpsychology.org.

Robyn Fivush, Marshall Duke, and Jennifer G. Bohanek, "'Do You Know . . .': The Power of Family History in Adolescent Identity and Well-Being," *Journal of Family Life*, February 23, 2010.

Describe the relationship patterns and estrangement history in your family and how this history has shaped your sibling relationships.

_____

_____

_____

_____

_____

_____

_____

_____

_____

_____

_____

_____

_____

_____

_____

Studies indicate that the reaction to ostracism is pain that thwarts the needs of belonging, self-esteem, control, and a meaningful existence. Describe all the ways you experience pain because of a cutoff with a sibling.

Have you sought "replacements" for estranged siblings, and how do these relationships fulfill you? In what ways do they fall short?

Chapter 9
Five Ways Estrangement Does Lifelong Damage
Some relationships are too toxic to sustain, but cutoffs may hurt well-being.

KEY POINTS

- Cutoffs can ripple through one's life and identity, producing a unique form of grief as the estranged mourn the living.
- The estranged often have a lingering difficulty adjusting to, accepting, and making sense of their losses.
- The estranged often suffer a loss of self-esteem and trust, which may play out in other relationships and ultimately compromise well-being.

Family estrangement causes ripples through one's life and identity. The experience creates a uniquely devastating form of grief in which an estranged family member often mourns the living.

The ambiguity of estrangement and the chronic hope (or dread) of encountering the estranged family member often exacerbate feelings of longing, anxiety, and anger. Those who are cut off often have a lingering difficulty adjusting to, accepting, and making sense of the loss, even when they have an otherwise fulfilling life. Those who choose to end a family relationship and consider it irrevocable may find that feelings of loss and regret accompany the decision.

Social-work researcher Kyle Agllias, one of the foremost experts on the subject, writes in her groundbreaking book, *Family Estrangement: A Matter of Perspective*, that estrangement is particularly difficult to accept because it has no predictable or predetermined outcomes nor an identifiable end point. "The death of a family member," she explains, "does not impact self-esteem or sense of self-worth the way estrangement does."

The loss is especially acute for siblings. Brothers and sisters are our earliest, closest companions. Losing what should have been a lifelong bond built on shared history is a sad, continuing deprivation.

In the survey I conducted for my first book, respondents discussed how the ongoing nature of estrangement defined their lives:

1. Trust

The estranged often feel they can't trust anyone, damaging their ability to fully engage in relationships. Several respondents described struggling with trust:

— *I actually find myself trying not to get too close to anybody because of my horrible experiences with family members who cut me out of their lives.*

— *I have major trust issues with everyone now. I worry that those I care about will suddenly leave me with no explanation.*

— *When a friend distances themselves from me for a good reason (a crisis where they need to be alone), I get triggered and panicked. I feel like I am being taken for granted as I did with my family.*

Author Agllias reports that estrangement-related trust issues can wreak such psychological havoc as emotional withdrawal, defensive posturing, people-pleasing behaviors, and overeager development of close but unsustainable relationships, possibly even leading to abuse.

2. Friendships

Without the ability to trust, developing friendships can be especially challenging. Worse, the estranged—especially those who initiated the cutoff—often feel judged and stigmatized when others have advised them to "forget about" the sibling or "move on." Some become needy and reliant on family and friends, imposing emotional demands and overblown expectations that can strain and even destroy relationships. "The estranged might feel a need to hold on tightly to non-estranged relationships for fear of losing them too," Agllias explains.

3. Self-esteem

One woman reported constantly questioning herself. She is socially reserved, feeling that if her own sister won't have a relationship with her, why would a mere acquaintance have any interest? She says she finds herself alone and isolated.

When a sibling terminates a relationship, the shunned sibling typically feels responsible for the breach. The loss leaves a gnawing sense of unlovability and lack of self-worth—typical of people who have been ostracized.

4. Family

Estrangement often places family members in the discomfiting and frequently impossible position of having to choose sides. The situation can become so polarizing as to incite a familial civil war. The estranged may aggressively recruit and lobby non-aligned family members, perhaps resorting to bullying, accusations, and attacks. The estranged may demand loyalty or threaten to ostracize family members who refuse to take their side.

My own mother felt caught between my brother and me when we were estranged. Here's how she recalls it:

> It was always in the back of my mind—I have a son and daughter who have nothing to do with each other. I was always thinking, What can I do? How can we get together? How can I get my family back? I felt hurt and embarrassed that my children didn't have anything to do with each other. I never talked to anyone about it. I felt ashamed, so I carried the pain alone.

> At times, I was furious about the situation: I would get invited to a family party that excluded one of my children. I never knew what to do—Should I attend or not? Should I insist that I will only go to an event if both my children are invited? Whatever choice I made, I was going to hurt one of my children.

5. Rumination

One of the most debilitating consequences of estrangement is the thought pattern of rumination: rehashing the same thoughts over and over, even when those thoughts breed sadness or negativity. Many rejected siblings—even some who chose to terminate the relationship—find themselves constantly mulling over what happened and why it happened. The mind is desperately trying to create meaning around an experience that may not have a good explanation. Chapter 15 explores ways to cope with rumination, which can be crippling, and over-sharing its bitter thoughts can drive people away.

Some relationships are simply too toxic to sustain. Still, there's no denying that cutoffs harm well-being and hurt other relationships. Awareness helps to guard against the long reach and lasting damage of estrangement.

REFERENCES

Agllias, Kylie (2017) *Family Estrangement: A Matter of Perspective* (New York: Routledge)

Williams, Kip, "Kip Williams Media Contact Overview," January 29, 2020, Social Psychology Network, williams.socialpsychology.org.

Loss of self-esteem is one of the most painful outcomes of sibling estrangement. Have you suffered with low self-esteem due to sibling estrangement? Give examples of situations where your low self-esteem is evident to you. What have you done to combat low self-esteem?

Do you struggle with trusting family and friends because of sibling estrangement? If a friend told you, "I can't trust family and friends because I don't feel I can trust my own brother sibling," how would you respond? What kind of advice would you give your friend?

How has sibling estrangement divided your family? How have some members taken sides? How do you think the family members who took sides should have handled this difficult situation? Can you discuss with family members how they handled the situation?

_____

_____

_____

_____

_____

_____

_____

_____

_____

_____

_____

_____

_____

_____

_____

_____

Chapter 10
Three Ways Siblings Stay Stuck in Toxic Relationships
Euphoric recall, future-faking, and self-gaslighting.

KEY POINTS

- Rosy memories and unrealistic hopes can keep a sibling in a toxic relationship.
- Know the words and tactics toxic siblings use and don't be blinded by enabling relatives who say things like, "Be the bigger person."
- Self-deceptive tactics may cause us to excuse bad behavior and to persuade ourselves to stay in the relationship.

Estrangement from a sibling can evoke deep, lasting mourning, not only for a relationship but also for the fantasy of the idealized family. Even siblings who are on good terms may recall a happier rapport in childhood, yearning to return to that simple, comfortable relationship. Adult brothers and sisters may be deeply disappointed, never having imagined they might become contentious, distant, or even estranged.

Rosy memories and unrealistic hopes can keep a sibling in a toxic relationship. Destructive thought patterns, such as euphoric recall, future-faking, and self-gaslighting, help us avoid facing the injuries a toxic sibling inflicts. These self-sabotaging beliefs can be the invisible glue that binds a sibling to a destructive relationship.

Cultural norms that present sibling relations as constant and enduring only add to the burden. Siblings who can't meet this expectation may feel coerced, judged, and stigmatized, both within and outside of the family.

Papering over a toxic relationship comes with insidious remarks like these:

- "Nobody's perfect."
- "You're too sensitive."
- "He didn't mean it that way."
- "You only have one brother/sister."
- "Can't you take a joke?"

- "You need to learn to let things go."
- "There are two sides to every story."
- "Why can't we all just get along?"
- "You shouldn't have made him angry."
- "Be the bigger person."

What Toxic Siblings Say and Do

Despite these pressures to keep up the connection, the reality is that some sibling relationships are dangerous, emotionally, and even physically. When abuse and/or violence occur, the relationship can't and shouldn't be sustained.

More typically, though, malice isn't so flagrant—and don't forget, toxic people often thrive on maintaining ambiguity. So, it's important to recognize red flags.

First, beware of a brother or sister telling you how to feel: This can indicate narcissism. Second, be alert to what they say, as toxic siblings often sprinkle their conversations with statements that subtly reinforce their control. You may recognize some examples:

- "We don't have secrets."
- "Look what you've done—gotten me into trouble with Mom/Dad."
- "I don't love you when you do that."
- "How can you think that? All I did was…"
- "And then he/she did this. I've got to do something about it—this is war."
- "How could you be so stupid?"
- "That didn't happen. You're making things up as usual."
- "You need to hear this."
- "You did this purposely."
- "You're trying to stir up trouble."
- "You'll regret that when I'm dead."
- "That's God's way of paying you back."
- "What would your friends think if they saw you now?"
- "These things only happen when you're around."

Toxic siblings also use various manipulative tactics:

- Blaming
- Being disrespectful
- Ignoring boundaries
- Triangulating
- Gaslighting
- Imposing the silent treatment

- Moving the goal posts
- Changing the subject
- Using fear to control another person
- Lying and denial
- Playing on a person's insecurities

Self-Deceptive Tactics That Keep Siblings in a Toxic Relationship

Even when siblings recognize manipulative statements and tactics, they're often reluctant to act, out of commitment to the family and the bonds of shared history. Some siblings find ways to excuse bad behavior, persuading themselves to stay in the relationship and rationalizing that choice.

Here are three self-deceptive tactics people may unwittingly employ:

1. **Euphoric recall:** This is a psychological process wherein people exaggerate happy memories and positive feelings while blocking out bad memories and the associated negative emotions. "This is a term that's often used in substance abuse," explains Canadian psychotherapist Ali-John Chaudhary, who specializes in sibling estrangement and conducts online sibling estrangement support groups. "I use the term 'fake nostalgia' to denote euphoric recall. Interestingly, this is a feeling that we can have when we're in the midst of thinking of our sibling relationship." Looking back through rose-colored glasses distorts past realities to prop up present-day optimism.

2. **Future-faking:** The playbook for future-faking is to promise that things will be better—or, at least, that things will change. It's a manipulative strategy a toxic sibling uses to get what they want right now, pressuring their sibling to excuse and overlook abuse. Typically, the toxic sibling claims that everything will be different when their life circumstances change and they're less stressed. Unfortunately, it's a lie. Think of the old bar sign that promises "Free Beer Tomorrow." Tomorrow, of course, never comes.

3. **Self-gaslighting:** This is an especially dangerous tactic because it is a self-inflicted form of emotional abuse. We dismiss our own valid emotions, instead accepting what a toxic sibling has said. Internalizing the toxic sibling's claims, we convince ourselves that we are "over-reacting" or "too sensitive" or "making a big a deal out of nothing." Minimization, invalidation, and self-doubt characterize self-gaslighting.

Recognizing these behaviors requires cultivating a "third eye"—that mystical, invisible eye, usually located on the forehead—that provides perception beyond ordinary eyesight. Siblings in toxic relationships must watch themselves from outside themselves to identify and defeat self-sabotaging behaviors.

Describe when you have fallen for future-faking with your estranged sibling. How did you believe things would change in the future? What actually happened?

_____

_____

_____

_____

_____

_____

_____

_____

_____

_____

_____

_____

_____

_____

Identify ways you gaslight yourself. What characteristics has your sibling assigned to you that you now accept as truth without question? Do you see yourself as the "golden child" or the "scapegoat" in the family? What roles do you tend to play in family relations?

Describe some of your childhood memories. Are they colored by euphoric recall? If so, try to remember and write in your inner child's voice how you felt when you had the original experience and how you felt about your sibling at that time.

_____

_____

_____

_____

_____

_____

_____

_____

_____

_____

_____

_____

_____

_____

Chapter 11

What to Do When Partners and Siblings Can't Get Along

... and when a partner is pressured to cut family ties.

KEY POINTS

- Siblings and new partners may feel jealous or threatened by each other.

- In some abusive situations, a partner may exert pressure on a sibling to cut family ties.

- A family may refuse to tolerate new partners who defy the family identity; they may reject someone on the basis of race, religion, or politics.

Sisters and brothers face one of the most perilous moments in their relationship when one of them chooses a life partner.

I didn't recognize the prevalence of this stress point until I conducted an informal survey for my first book. Many respondents blamed a spouse or partner for fracturing a sibling relationship. Some of their comments are bitter and painful:

— *My brother's wife has tons of drama and hate in her life. I am 100 percent positive she is the precipitating factor.*

— *She met her boyfriend and he slowly started cutting out everyone until he had manipulated her into interacting with him only. I pray I never run into him because I may pulverize him.*

— *My brother's wife values status, money, and connections above all else. I have none of these things, so I am not useful.*

Any new relationship presents challenging questions: *How will this person fit into our family? Is she or he anything like other family members? Can I cultivate warm relations with the new addition?*

"Our brothers and sisters were our first 'marriage' partners," says Karen Gail Lewis, author of *Siblings: The Ghosts of Childhood That Haunt Your Love and Work*. "We have a lot of emotional stock invested in them and in the spouses they choose."

Partners May Feel Possessive

A new partner may feel threatened by, or jealous of, closeness between brothers and sisters. Siblings, especially those close in age, may find themselves experiencing the same emotions, particularly if they're not in a relationship. The "left behind" sibling may feel shut out and resentful. To assuage these feelings, the new partner—or the sibling—would do well to identify and cultivate a shared interest that can pave the way for connection.

But some cases are impossible. The partner, always in the sibling's ear, can wield a powerful influence and may use it against the family. A new spouse may initiate a crusade against their in-laws immediately after the wedding. If the couple doesn't strive for even-handed treatment—electing, for example, to attend one family's holiday celebration over the other's—a rift can develop quickly. When perceived as a snub, favoritism can lead to deep resentments.

Over time, even a subtle campaign can erode once-strong sibling relationships. In extreme cases, a partner may irrationally begrudge his or her partner's childhood experiences, friends, and family—everything before he or she appeared on the scene. Such a partner may force an uncomfortable choice: "Your family or me."

"If it comes down to my wife or my sister," said one brother who has endured these pressures, "I'm going to choose my wife, since that's who I'm living with every day."

Is This Abuse?

Exerting pressure to sever family ties can be a dangerous sign of partner or spousal abuse. A controlling partner typically establishes dominance through demands: requiring frequent check-ins, insisting that the couple do everything together, etc. Gradually, the controlling partner weakens the other and, ultimately, even when someone comes to recognizes what's happening to them, they may already feel isolated and unable to confide in anyone; he or she has been left lacking a support system at a time of urgent need.

One man described how his first marriage led to an emotional estrangement from his sister and widowed mother: "My first wife seemed to feel that if I had a relationship with my mother and sister, it would diminish my relationship with her," he says. "It was difficult to visit my mom and sister, especially with my wife. It seemed we were all looking at the clock, waiting for the visit to end."

Some Families Reject New Members

On the other hand, a new partner may encounter a hostile reception from their in-laws. If the family finds a newcomer to be demanding or difficult—or just doesn't like him or her—they may shun the couple entirely. A strong-willed family may refuse to tolerate traits that diverge from or defy the family identity, such as race, sexual orientation, religious differences, political beliefs, or unconventional career choices. Psychologist Mark Sichel, director of the Addiction Recovery Unit at Hebrew Union College in New York and the author of *Healing from Family Rifts*, explains that, to keep a family identity intact, members often assert shared values and discourage individual differences. They may go so far as to cast out anyone challenging the family identity through their lifestyle choices.

Knowingly or not, some people choose a partner willing to take on the dirty work of cutting off the family. Prince Harry of England, who married far outside his family identity, may have found in American actress Meghan Markle a partner to help him establish distance—even a near-total break—from his family. As he has said, until he met Markle, "I was trapped, but I didn't know it."

Who's to Blame?

Convenient as it may be to blame the new partner for disrupting family relationships, it's important to recognize that they rarely are solely responsible for the estrangement.

"My brother's wife is a very manipulative individual," says one woman who is estranged from her only brother. "I put up with a lot for a long time, for the sake of a relationship with my brother. But my mental health was deteriorating, and I finally confronted him. He did not respond. I quit blaming her for his behaviors because he is an adult." She has had to accept that her brother's tolerance of his partner's manipulative behavior tacitly supports their estrangement.

It's a cruel irony: The selection of a life partner—with whom an individual shares the greatest intimacy — can result in profound hurts and deep divisions in the family of origin.

In your family life, what techniques have you used to reduce conflict or resolve differences? How successful have these techniques been for you? Describe a time when a partner or in-law exacerbated or helped to resolve sibling estrangement.

_____

_____

_____

_____

_____

_____

_____

_____

_____

_____

_____

_____

_____

_____

Do you consider your race, gender, sexual orientation, class status, income level or any other identifier to be a factor in your estrangement with your sibling? In other words, have you strayed from "the family myth"? If so, please describe.

Describe a time or times when you have experienced jealousy towards a sibling. What is the belief you hold about yourself that is behind this feeling? How did you resolve some of your feelings of jealousy?

Chapter 12
The Five Stages of Grief for an Estranged Sibling
Grieving a sibling relationship is (and isn't) like mourning a death.

KEY POINTS

- The five stages of grief for those estranged from a sibling are different from Elisabeth Kübler-Ross's five stages of grief for a death.

- Sibling estrangement often results in an ambiguous loss, causing a brother or sister to mourn without ever finding resolution.

- The estranged often ruminate, fixating on their loss and searching for some way to gain insight or solve the problem.

Psychologist Elisabeth Kübler-Ross, named by *Time Magazine* as one of the "100 Most Important Thinkers of the 20th Century," identified the five stages of grief after death as denial, anger, bargaining, depression, and acceptance. (*Note: After experiencing someone's death, not all of the five stages of grief may be experienced or in the same order.*)

Kübler-Ross made an important advance simply by organizing the inchoate process of grieving into a coherent set of psychological stages—an act that helps to make the unimaginable manageable. With some adjustment, the stages she identified can well apply to the plight of the estrangee—one who has been cut off. For the estrangee, the (often overlapping) stages of grief are the following:

- **Confusion:** Often, a sibling simply doesn't understand the reasons for the cutoff.

- **Anger:** Siblings typically expect their relationship will last a lifetime, and they feel betrayed and abandoned when the cutoff occurs.

- **Helplessness:** The estranged have no voice or agency when their siblings refuse to acknowledge them.
- **Depression:** Feelings of loss and helplessness lead directly to depression, especially as the sense of family belonging dwindles.
- **Rumination:** Unique to grieving a sibling relationship, many estrangees find themselves caught in "loop" thinking, unable to control destructive thought patterns.

It's difficult to accept that someone you love is walking the earth who wants absolutely nothing to do with you. Many respondents to the survey I conducted for my book, *Brothers, Sisters, Strangers: Sibling Estrangement and the Road to Reconciliation*, characterized the loss of a sibling relationship as worse than a death in the family. They used vivid words and images to capture their chronic feelings of emptiness.

— *Estrangement is like a bad tooth that's always pulsating with pain.*

— *Sibling estrangement is a wound that never heals.*

— *After 25 years of no contact with my sister, I am still waiting for the hurting to stop.*

Ambiguous Loss

Estrangement can create what's called an ambiguous loss when a loved one still exists physically but is missing emotionally. Those who mourn someone who is still alive often keep that person present psychologically in the hope that one day that person might reappear.

Divorce, a loved one gone missing, and emigration to another country all are situations in which ambiguous loss can arise. Here, it occurs when a sibling relationship ends even though the brother or sister is very much alive and, often, orbiting in social circles close to ours.

The difficulty comes from the hope that the relationship may somehow be rekindled; therefore, the process of grieving and recovering from the loss is never resolved. We experience all the emotions of grieving without ever reaching resolution.

Adding insult to injury, in time, bereft sisters and brothers who have been cut off may discover that they also are excluded from many family events. In my survey, the list is long and includes the following:

- A party to celebrate a 60th wedding anniversary
- A mother's retirement party, which included a family gathering before the main event
- A young nephew's birthday party
- A sister's wedding
- A nationwide search for a niece who went missing

Psychologist Pauline Boss, Professor Emeritus in the Department of Family Social Science at the University of Minnesota, explains that those caught in ambiguous loss, like estrangees, are stuck on a Mobius strip of rumination and in a constant state of bereavement. She writes that their emotions can "fluctuate between hope and hopelessness. Suffered too long, these emotions can deaden feeling and make it impossible for people to move on with their lives." She explains that it is difficult to live with what she calls "two truths"—for example, my brother, who wants nothing to do with me, is still my brother. This state of limbo thwarts the grieving process, making ambiguous loss one of the hardest losses to accept.

Rumination

Consequently, some of the estranged—both estrangees and estrangers—ruminate. Their minds fixate on a single thought or string of thoughts, typically sad or dark, relentlessly repeating in a futile effort to gain insight into the problem.

This thought pattern is one of the most distinct and difficult aspects of sibling estrangement. Respondents to my survey referred to this "loop"—the inability to move forward—in their answers:

— *I think about my sister all the time. I'm shattered that we are not part of each other's lives for so many years.*

— *My head goes round and round about the things that have happened.*

— *I can't stop thinking about the estrangement, and the pain is agonizing.*

Confusion, helplessness, and rumination don't appear in Kübler-Ross's stages of grief. Of these, the most important difference is rumination, which displaces acceptance. Chapter 15 explores ways to cope with rumination.

Death is final, and therefore easier to accept, explains one woman who has been estranged from her sister for two years. "This is worse," she says. "They're out there, you know where they live, you know their number, but they don't want you in their life."

REFERENCES

Boss, Pauline (2000). *Ambiguous Loss: Learning to Live with Unresolved Grief.* Harvard University Press

If you feel you are grieving your estranged sibling, do you also grieve a part of yourself? Describe what you feel you have lost—a sense of who you are, a role, an intact family.

_____

_____

_____

_____

_____

_____

_____

_____

_____

_____

_____

_____

_____

_____

Do you find yourself experiencing confusion, anger, helplessness, depression, and rumination due to sibling estrangement? Do you feel stuck in one of these emotions? Please describe. How are you able to mitigate these feelings?

One of the troubling results of sibling estrangement is the process of "rumination." Identify the thoughts and words that repeat in your mind. How has rumination affected your life and well-being?

_____

_____

_____

_____

_____

_____

_____

_____

_____

_____

_____

_____

_____

_____

_____

_____

Coping with Sibling Estrangement

Chapter 13
Should You Reconcile with an Estranged Sibling?
Estranged siblings may want to reconcile, many due to the pandemic. Here's how.

KEY POINTS

- Studies show that more than 40 percent of people experience family estrangement at some point in their lives.
- Reconciliation can be risky, so it's important to carefully evaluate whether to re-enter a relationship with a difficult sibling.
- There are no hard and fast rules on how to reconcile—or whether it's even necessary to discuss the roots of the cutoff.

"I just talked to Scott. He's unbelievably upset. I don't know. I don't know what to do…"

I was stunned when I listened to this terrified voicemail from my 89-year-old mother. She was talking about my older brother—whom I hadn't spoken to in decades—begging me to contact him and help him out of a dark place of illness and despair.

After clicking off my mother's frantic message, I re-introduced myself to the concept of a sibling. "My brother," I said out loud. He had been out of my life for so long that I didn't even remember why we were apart.

Now, my mother's desperate request raised profound questions. *What is my responsibility to my brother when we've had no relationship for years? What is my responsibility to the family…to my mother? How can I trust my brother, who has repeatedly hurt and betrayed me?*

To Reconcile or Not to Reconcile

Studies show that more than 40 percent of people have experienced family estrangement at some point in their lives. During the pandemic, many found themselves weighing whether to try to reconcile. Aware of their own mortality, some feared that if they didn't contact an estranged family member now, they might not ever have the chance.

To approach reconciliation in a rational, self-protective, yet open fashion, it's crucial to assess one's own feelings and the prospects for the relationship. Consider the following questions:

- Why is this relationship important to me—not to my family, or to anyone else, but to me?

- Does my family member want to resume a relationship?

- Can I set aside the anger, pain, and/or resentment that led to the break to change our pattern of relating?

- Do I want to resume this relationship even if I discover that neither of us has changed?

- What needs to be different to create a genuine relationship? (Identifying these needs helps each sibling establish boundaries for a renewed relationship.)

- Will I compromise too much of myself if I try to sustain a relationship with my difficult family member?

To Discuss or Not to Discuss

There are no rules on how to approach reconciling. Some people simply pick up a relationship without even discussing the past or the events that drove them apart. Other estranged siblings fear that they'll continue to harbor resentments if they never discuss the source of their problems.

When they were in their 20s, Leah Barr of Naples, Florida, and her older brother stopped talking to each other. The two, now in their 60s, have never discussed the issues that fueled their estrangement. At the time of the cutoff, both had young children, and the families would alternate having Christmas and Thanksgiving dinners at each other's houses.

Suddenly, one year, Leah's brother didn't invite her family to the holiday dinner at his home. That seemed to be the catalyst. Afterward, when they attended a family gathering, the two would avoid each other. In time, the divide spread to other family members.

After six years, Leah says, the two finally spoke again at their mother's funeral:

> My brother and I looked at one another over her casket and said to each other that it was horrible our 59-year-old mother went to her grave thinking that two of her children were not talking. I swore I would never have another divide, even if it meant eating crow. I never want to hurt others in that way.

Yet, without an understanding of the causes, Leah says she never feels close to him. For a long time, she feared they would lapse back into estrangement:

> I don't know if I fully trust him because I don't understand what the issue was then. How can I correct my own actions if I don't know what I did wrong? And it's hard to fully commit to someone when they've betrayed you in a fundamental way.

Leah describes their current relationship as an amicable cease-fire, but she has no sense of peace.

How to Approach an Estranged Sibling

To promote understanding and reconciliation, estranged family members would benefit from:

- Sitting down together, face to face.
- Listening without interrupting, and without challenging each other's stories. Seek understanding. Reconciliation is impossible without true, genuine listening.
- Acknowledging, with empathy, the other person's hurt, anger, or alienation—even if it doesn't make sense to you. Assume they have sincere, trustworthy intentions. When each party accepts the other's experiences, neither feels devalued nor shut out.
- Letting go of anger.
- Emphasizing consistently your hope of creating a mutual bond—and your willingness to work at it.

My Reconciliation with My Brother After a 40-Year Estrangement

After that desperate message from our mother, I made the difficult decision to reach out to my brother. In many challenging but worthwhile conversations over the course of a year, we explored the reasons for the cutoff while rebuilding our relationship. I captured our emotional journey in my book *Brothers, Sisters, Strangers: Sibling Estrangement and the Road to Reconciliation.*

I wrote the book with my brother's permission to share our story, and he wrote the afterword to offer his perspective. Even now, it's deeply moving for me to read some of what he wrote: "We grew up together and we went through a lot during those years. My sister probably knows me better than anyone. I feel balanced that we have a relationship again...I don't have the relationship I'd like with my niece and nephews. I can't change the past, but at least I know I'll always have a sister."

Our mother, now 96, couldn't be happier that we've reconciled. The work of reuniting would have been worth it for that alone. Even better, for my brother and me, there's now a sense of peace where there was once only hurt and longing.

What would reconciliation look like for you? What kind of relationship do you hope to have? Explore whether your expectations are realistic. Have you attempted to reconcile? If so, what precipitated the attempt and how did it go?

_____

_____

_____

_____

_____

_____

_____

_____

_____

_____

_____

_____

_____

_____

_____

_____

Create a "T chart" on the topic of reconciliation with an estranged sibling. Entitle the left-hand column "Benefits" and list all the positive aspects of reconciliation. Entitle the right-hand column "Drawbacks" and list the negative prospects of reconciliation.

If there has been a reconciliation, have you ever discussed the issues between you and your sibling? Do you feel it's necessary to explore what happened and how it made you feel? Can you reconcile without a discussion of past issues and events? What would be gained by this discussion?

Chapter 14

Staying Connected to Siblings When You Hate Their Politics

Learning to say, "I disagree, but respect you" at holiday gatherings.

KEY POINTS

- Intense political views can shatter a sibling bond.

- Typically, siblings spend more time together than anyone else, and their relationships can outlast friendships and marriages.

- Calm words can defuse the most explosive moments in a sibling relationship.

A blunt social media post, a slip on the family text thread, a careless remark during a holiday celebration.

The slightest offense can shatter a sibling bond made brittle by partisan opinions in these intensely political times. Beliefs are built on values, and family foundations often crack around political fissures.

Stacy Washington, host of *Stacy on the Right* on SiriusXM Patriot Channel 125, said many of her listeners are suffering from estrangement due to divergent political views within the family.

She interviewed me on a recent program and asked, "What should they do?"

Divergent Political Views as a Risk Factor for Estrangement

Many respondents to my survey identified divergent political views as a common reason for a sibling cutoff.

Here are a few their comments:

— *It all started after 9/11 when my brother said he wanted to kill all Muslims. When Trump was elected, he amped up his anti-Dem rhetoric. Recently, I had to unfriend him on Facebook when he posted, "Death to all Democrats."*

— *The politics of the times—to vax or not to vax, to mask or not to mask, to educate at school or home—are strangling the relationships in our family.*

— *I couldn't be my authentic self around my brother because we disagree politically on masks, vaccines, and guns. I was always avoiding topics, and eventually, we avoided each other.*

Why Siblings Matter

As discussed earlier, humans have a fundamental need to belong. Absent a sense of belonging—a feeling of emotional safety and context—people come to fear that their very lives are at risk.

Even when estrangement is a clearheaded choice to shut the door on unbearable discord, the cutoff often leaves disconnected siblings stranded in shame. In time, estranged siblings lose their defining family identities: big brother or little sister, uncle or aunt, brother-in-law or sister-in-law. Their children suffer the loss of an extended family, lacking even a cousin or two with whom to whisper secrets, vex their parents, and mark life's milestones.

Sibling rejection can also have devastating personal consequences, rippling into many parts of life and identity: It affects self-esteem—who you are and how you see yourself—your friendships and other social relationships, your well-being and ability to trust, and your family members as they choose sides. Chapter 7 explores some of these consequences.

How to Stay Connected When Family Members Find Each Other's Politics Repugnant

Here was my advice:

- Seek common ground in shared experiences and memories to rise above political differences.
- Avoid contentious topics. If you find your sibling's politics offensive, restrict, or block social media accounts.
- Have an exit strategy when conversations become tense.
- Place a priority on children. For example, to protect children, a family might agree to wear masks at an indoor gathering because that's what's best for the little ones.
- Request a matriarch or patriarch enforce a moratorium on politics at family events. The enforcer should immediately shut down raised voices, profanity, and personal insults.

The estranged might write an email to estranged siblings, emphasizing their desire to re-establish relations, and proposing parameters for their relationships—i.e., banning certain topics. To encourage dialogue and draw up a sibling relationship contract, ask relatives for suggestions on how the family can be together.

Even though my brother's and my issues are not political, I often remind myself that we need not concur on everything, and it's not my job to change his mind. I've learned to say, "I disagree, but I respect your viewpoint," and "you've given me something to think about. Can we talk about this some other time?"

These simple words defuse the most explosive moment. They're the wisdom won after a separation that cost our family dearly. Now, years into our reconciliation, the gratitude and connection my brother and I share is a treasure for our elderly mother and our children.

For us, as for many siblings who have overcome estrangement—whether rooted in old, cold slights or today's red-hot politics—the loving presence of a brother or sister is its reward.

Describe how political issues have interfered with your sibling relationship. Can you reflect on the techniques you've discovered that reduce the strain of political differences?

_____

_____

_____

_____

_____

_____

_____

_____

_____

_____

_____

_____

_____

_____

What activities did you share in childhood with your sibling? At what point did you notice a fraying of your bond with your sibling? Is it possible for you to limit your relationship to activities that bring both of you joy and avoid topics in conversation that divide you?

Of the suggestions offered to facilitate sibling reconciliation, which have you attempted and what level of success did you experience? In what ways can you build upon your successes?

_____

_____

_____

_____

_____

_____

_____

_____

_____

_____

_____

_____

_____

Chapter 15

Ten Ways to Stop Ruminating

8. Identify your triggers.

KEY POINTS

- The mind seeks an answer or meaning in any experience. Consequently, people try to think through an experience to better understand a problem.

- The average brain generates 15,000 to 50,000 thoughts in a day, and most are negative.

- Studies show that a 90-minute walk in nature or a single session of exercise can reduce symptoms of rumination.

One of the most plaguing consequences of sibling estrangement is the thought pattern of rumination: rehashing the same thoughts, over and over, even when those thoughts breed sadness or negativity. Many rejected siblings—and even some who chose to terminate the relationship—find themselves constantly mulling over, "*What did I do? What was my role in the cutoff? Can I fix this?*"

Why Do People Ruminate?

"We are natural problem solvers," explains Canadian psychotherapist Ali-John Chaudhary. "The mind will seek out an answer or a sense of meaning in any experience. People assume that if they think through an issue, they'll better understand it and resolve it."

Some people ruminate as a result of previous trauma. Those prone to depression may get stuck in "loop" thinking, perpetuating a sense of blame and shame, exacerbating a negative mental state.

"In the worst cases," Chaudhary says, "rumination can contribute to isolation. Dwelling on the negative, constantly discussing bitter thoughts with others, can drive people away."

As one woman who is estranged from her sibling said, "Rumination can cripple people mentally and cause a lot of anxiety and self-gaslightig."

Those who self-gaslight frequently internalize abuse to which they've been subjected, convincing themselves that their tormentor's perceptions are accurate. They're unable to "turn off" doubt-inducing thoughts running insistently through their mind. "Maybe things weren't so bad," they may think. Or, "S/he didn't really mean that." Or, "Maybe I deserve to be treated like this."

Even when a ruminating person recognizes that these thought patterns are self-destructive, they don't know how to stop. Many feel they're hostages of their own negative thoughts, yet they lack the tools to free themselves.

Stopping the Pattern Takes Discipline.

Here are some effective ways to derail rumination:

1. **Find a way to distract yourself.** Call a friend—and talk about anything but the thoughts troubling you. Exercise, tackle some chores, work on a puzzle, watch a movie, or spend time in nature. A 2014 study found that after a 90-minute nature walk, people reported fewer symptoms of rumination. And a 2018 study determined that a single session of exercise reduced symptoms of rumination. Try for optimal results by combining exercise with time outdoors.

2. **Make an action plan** for doing what you can to address the problem. Determine what you can control and write down your ideas to emphasize their importance.

3. **Move forward by taking one of the actions you've identified.**

4. **Challenge your own thinking.** Ask yourself if your troubling thoughts are accurate. The National Science Foundation reports that the average brain generates 15,000 to 50,000 thoughts daily. Most are negative, and up to 90 percent are repetitive. These Automatic Negative Thoughts (ANTs) can cause chronic stress, even changing your brain chemistry by depleting "feel-good" neurotransmitters (serotonin and dopamine). Consciously replace ANTs with positive affirmations, even if you feel silly at first. Building positive habits is an important aspect of self-care.

5. **Adjust your life goals,** perhaps reducing expectations of yourself and others.

6. **Enhance self-esteem** by building upon existing strengths, or sample new activities to discover where you can excel. Poor self-esteem is closely associated with increased rumination.

7. **Meditation** can reduce rumination by promoting a calm emotional state and grounding you in the present moment. It also helps identify the connection between thoughts and feelings. When you catch

yourself ruminating, sit down, breathe deeply, and focus just on your breathing.

8. **Identify—and then avoid—your triggers.** When you start ruminating, note where you are, the time of day, who's around you, and what you've been doing. In today's world, even watching the news or scrolling through social media may be triggers. A "diet" restricting news and social media can help.

9. **Set a timer.** Allow yourself to feel disturbing emotions for a set period. Then place a rubber band around your wrist. Each time you find yourself returning to negative thoughts, snap the rubber band. This will make you more aware of your repetitious thought patterns.

10. **Consider therapy** - If rumination becomes too intense, you may want to work with a therapist to help identify the core issues that are fueling rumination.

As Buddha said, "Nothing can harm you as much as your own thoughts." Those who ruminate know the deep truth of this statement—and the wisdom of acting on it.

REFERENCES

Bratman, Gregory N., (2015) "Nature experience reduces rumination and subgenual prefrontal cortex activation," *PNAS*, Volume 112. No. 28

Brand, Serge, (2018) "Acute Bouts of Exercising Improved Mood, Rumination and Social Interaction in Inpatients with Mental Disorders," *Frontiers in Psychology,* Published online 2018 Mar 13. doi: 10.3389/fpsyg.2018.00249

To what extent have you ruminated about your estrangement? How did rumination affect your well-being?

_____

_____

_____

_____

_____

_____

_____

_____

_____

_____

_____

_____

_____

_____

_____

Rumination and self-blame often go hand-in-hand as a consequence of sibling estrangement. Create a T-chart with two columns. In the first column, record the thoughts and words that loop through your mind when you ruminate. In the second column, make the case for why these thoughts are not true.

Which of the ten suggested techniques to halt rumination have you attempted? Why did you select these techniques? Try to apply these techniques over the course of one day and record here how you felt after modifying your behavior.

_____

_____

_____

_____

_____

_____

_____

_____

_____

_____

_____

_____

_____

Chapter 16
A New Holiday Tradition for the Estranged: Quit Social Media

During the holidays, some connections rub salt in old wounds of the estranged.

KEY POINTS

- Social media can be hurtful for the estranged, especially during the holidays.
- "Perfect" social media posturing creates a fake reality that can deepen real emotional damage.
- Exposure to images of estranged family members can disrupt the grieving process and set back healing.

For those hurting from a cutoff with a sibling, the holidays may be the ideal time to shut off social media apps. You'll spare yourself the hurt of exclusion from holiday gatherings.

The world of social media can be dangerous territory for the estranged. Browsing on social media during the holidays carries a heightened risk of jealousy and FOMO (fear of missing out). Many users, after viewing photos of other "happy" families, feel envious. For the estranged, those festive images can be particularly unsettling.

"My friends post pictures with all their sisters, husbands, and children having a get-together," says Julianna Turner, a 54-year-old Scottish Latina who hasn't spoken to her brother and sister in five years. "I scroll through the same pictures for hours. It looks so fun and heartwarming. I'm crushed that I will never have that."

"Perfect" Lives on Social Media

No matter how intense their longing, the estranged aren't likely to find satisfying or accurate information on social media. Facebook, Instagram, Twitter, and similar "sharing" outlets tend to be more about posturing than connecting, says Dr. Brian A. Primack, dean of the College of Public Health and Human Sciences at Oregon State University. He has conducted research on the effects of media messages and technological advances on health.

Users distill their activities into a few words and photos, consciously displaying themselves in the most positive light. Many aim to create a carefully designed, "perfect" social media version of their "perfect" lives. "Even though it seems like the people you are interacting with are very 'real,'" Primack says, "their messages and feeds are in fact very highly curated."

Even worse, exposure to an estranged sibling's posts, "likes," comments and photos, whether direct or indirect (through a relative's or mutual friend's feed), can be like picking at scabs, preventing emotional wounds from healing, and inhibiting the grieving process.

Longing for Connection, Even at a Distance

Brothers and sisters who have experienced lengthy cutoffs often are curious to see what family members now look like, especially during the holidays, when they have time on their hands. They wonder how everyone else is celebrating this year. Social media provides a window—albeit an opaque, one-sided one—through which to view loved ones. Though there's no opportunity to develop these relationships, the estranged may feel some connection from observing relatives in photos or videos. Almost inevitably, these images reinforce the painful reality that family members are physically present but psychologically absent.

A platform for Reconciliation — or a New Battleground?

Social media becomes even darker when feuding relatives use the platforms as an additional battleground. Knowing a disowned family member is watching, some will intentionally post hurtful entries, consciously worsening hostility and hurt between themselves and their estranged sibling. Some escape this cruel game by blocking all family members from their social media accounts.

The estranged who are hoping for some sort of reconciliation via social media often are disappointed, partly because of the nature of the medium. People treat one another differently online than they might in a face-to-face encounter. Social media has a quality of remove; it's less personal, and users don't worry as much about hurting others' feelings. Social media just isn't conducive to in-depth discussion, especially one that might lead to healing a troubled relationship.

While social media can be a space where rifts spread to other family members, these platforms also may help contain the cancer of estrangement. Parents, nieces, nephews, and others caught in the crossfire may reach out privately on social media to maintain some connection, even if the estranged aren't attending family events. For those who find their relationships becoming collateral damage to sibling estrangement, these contacts may help reduce feelings of isolation.

Susanna Garth, a Pacific Islander who grieves estrangement from her elder and only sister, understands the peril of habitually glimpsing her sister, niece, and nephew via social media. Garth doesn't understand why her sister cut her off and lived for years in hopes that things would change.

Instead, Facebook dealt her another blow. A year ago, she was shocked and hurt to discover that her sister's husband had blocked her from his page. She then recognized that the Facebook stream of family pictures and posts had taken a terrible toll.

"I need space to grieve," she says. "I have decided to block my sister so she can't find my profile. Hanging on to what was is not healthy for me."

Is Social Media Worth the Risk?

Estranged siblings must carefully weigh the perils of social media. If an estranged sibling is aggressive, it might be best to avoid these platforms as a potential battleground. But, if users can tolerate feelings of exclusion and jealousy that an estranged sibling's posts could trigger, social media can offer a thread of a connection to that branch of the family.

Users may ask themselves:

- How hostile is my estranged sister or brother?
- Is he or she likely to lash out at me on these platforms?
- How well-adjusted am I to the estrangement?
- Can I tolerate some exposure to my sibling's life, or will those encounters disturb my ability to accept the cutoff?

For Susanna and others who are estranged, social media may seem to offer an opportunity to recapture a sibling relationship—especially during the holidays, when feelings of loss are acute. Yet its use may keep the wound open and raw, perpetuating the turmoil and relentless sadness of mourning the living.

Do you follow your sibling on social media? If so, how does that affect you? Can you describe a situation where you were excluded or hurt by your siblings on social media?

Describe how your sibling presents himself or herself on social media. Is it an accurate portrayal? In what ways has social media presented a distilled view of other family members?

In what ways has social media intensified the divide in your relationship with your sibling? What would be the fallout if you were to block your sibling or stop using social media entirely?

_____

_____

_____

_____

_____

_____

_____

_____

_____

_____

_____

_____

_____

_____

_____

Chapter 17
Why Holidays Are So Hard for Those Who Are Estranged
... and 8 ways to gain greater perspective and peace.

KEY POINTS

- Those in fractured families often dread Christmas hype and the long, melancholy season that they may spend alone.
- Family estrangement is an epidemic, with one survey suggesting that as many as 67 million Americans live with family rifts.
- Lowering expectations and reframing the holiday experience can help the estranged cope with end-of-year blues.

The fantasy of the perfect American holiday is captured in one of Norman Rockwell's most famous portraits. In it an ideal American family of eleven people spanning three generations is seated around the Thanksgiving table, beaming at one another and at a bounteous spread of food. This 1943 painting set the standard for what we think our holidays should look like: joyful kin of all ages, basking in the warmth, comfort, and love of family.

This, however, is not the holiday scene awaiting the estranged. Those cut off from family feel their losses acutely from October through December, and the aggressive spread of holiday cheer only worsens the suffering: Even a well-meaning "Happy Holidays! Hope you're enjoying time with your family" can twist the knife.

During the years when I was estranged from my only brother, I struggled to get through the holidays. From the lavish downtown decorations to the local grocery store's tinsel, every bright, jingling holiday display reminded me of the "happy family" I was missing. Things seemed to get worse every year, with retailers nudging profits forward until candy canes jumped Halloween altogether and began popping up as part of back-to-school sales.

When the big days finally arrived, I scrambled to fill the chairs at my holiday table. Year after year, I cooked the usual elaborate feast for just a few people.

Worst of all, I assumed I was the only one suffering from the alienation, pain, and stigma of being shunned. Amid everyone else's togetherness, I felt terribly alone.

Alone in Aloneness?

I was reluctant to join a support group or even to share my story. I didn't talk about the hole that estrangement had dug into my life because I feared I would be judged. People tend to project onto others their own notions of what a family should look like, and society cherishes an idealized version of family in which relationships are indissoluble.

So, when I began working on a book about sibling estrangement, I found that I was not alone. I interviewed experts and conducted a survey asking for estranged siblings' stories, and I learned that most people don't want to talk about living in a fractured family—one of life's most painful experiences. Many refuse to fill out surveys, making it difficult to determine how many people are estranged. Karl Pillemer's research for his book, *Fault Lines: Fractured Families and How to Mend Them*, revealed that 67 million Americans have family rifts. It's an epidemic.

I learned from my interviews that many of the estranged suffer from greater depression, loneliness, and low self-worth as the weather turns cold.

"Fall sucks," a woman who doesn't talk to her siblings said bluntly. "I say it every year. The holidays rub your face in the estrangement."

Some said that they wake up crying in their sleep, devastated by their losses. Even some who *chose* to sever family relations found that holidays spent alone could prompt a reevaluation of whether a cutoff was the right choice.

For Some, It's Not a Time of Mourning

Others actually said they felt relieved that they don't have to endure strained gatherings with "loved ones." Yet even for them, there's no graceful answer to the question every acquaintance seems to ask: "What are you doing for the holidays?"

Some of the estranged are remarkably resilient. One woman who doesn't talk to her sister said she reframed her holiday experiences by focusing on what she doesn't miss about family gatherings. The list includes an uncle's incessant political diatribes, drunk relatives, a brother's cutting remarks, and her sister's dry stuffing.

Others, however, spoke of fearing the isolation of holidays without family. One woman rejoiced when she received a coveted invitation for a holiday dinner with friends. She said she felt as if she'd won the lottery because she would escape the sadness she typically feels on that day.

Things to Do on Lonely Days

For those who have no place to go but home, it's natural to dread the dreary, lonely days. Here are a few suggestions:

- **Decorate your home just as you like.** Then think ahead to make specific plans for the days you'll be alone. Consider entertainment, like a concert or a visit to a botanical garden; or prepare special dishes, just for you.

- **Volunteer to help at a crisis center for homeless people, refugees, or others in need.** Surround yourself with people who, unlike family, may appreciate your time and efforts.

- **To address your spiritual side, go to a religious service, maybe even of a different religion.** Plan a peaceful day focused on appreciating what you have rather than dwelling on what's missing.

- **Take a walk to see the local lights.** Every culture has celebrated a holiday that brings light to the darkest days of the year.

- **Don't feel obligated to spend the holidays as one "should."** This time is yours. Do what you wish. Take a trip, organize closets, do projects you've put off. Or give in to simple pleasures like binge-watching TV, reading, and eating meals when you want to.

- **Start new traditions to make the holidays less stressful and more fun.**

- **Avoid letting technology sprinkle salt on your wounds.** Mute or delete social media apps during the holidays. You might even decide to leave them for good.

- **Assess what you're missing.** Maybe you're grateful that you don't have to deal with family drama.

A fractured family is reason enough for the estranged to say, "Bah humbug!" They may wish the calendar would fast-forward to January, allowing them to skip the holiday madness, mark the New Year, and put off another round of suffering for 10 months. That being impossible, what *is* possible is to make your own holiday cheer, and to find peace when you can, where you can.

In the fall months, have you found yourself distressed and dreading the winter holidays? Describe some of your feelings. What can you do to reduce your distress?

_____

_____

_____

_____

_____

_____

_____

_____

_____

_____

_____

_____

_____

_____

What are some techniques you are willing to try to lower holiday expectations? What does "reframing the holiday experience" mean to you? What actions could you take to reframe a particular holiday?

Have you found sibling substitutes after the estrangement? If yes, please describe. Can you gather with them for the holidays? What plans have you made in anticipation of upcoming family holidays?

_____

_____

_____

_____

_____

_____

_____

_____

_____

_____

_____

_____

_____

_____

_____

Chapter 18
How to Mourn an Estranged Sibling Relationship
Finding meaning and learning to tolerate uncertainty.

KEY POINTS

- Estrangement is a non-event—indefinite, open-ended, often unexplained—and an ambiguous loss, an enduring absence without closure.

- The estranged often fluctuate between hope and hopelessness, desire and despair.

- Moving on requires finding meaning in the loss, learning to tolerate uncertainty, and discovering new hope.

"How do I move on, and not have sibling estrangement affect my life through a constant emotional ache?"

A reader posed this frequently asked question last week. It's undoubtedly the most vexing, most persistent problem the estranged face: *How do I mourn the loss of my sibling relationship?*

Grieving an estrangement is never an easy process, especially for the rejected. It's difficult to accept that someone you love, someone you expected would accompany you through life, still walks the Earth—but wants nothing to do with you.

Essentially, sibling estrangement requires mourning a living person. Unlike in death, however, this mourning process fails to bring acceptance and gradual recovery. We experience all the emotions of grieving but can't reach a resolution.

Estrangement is a non-event: indefinite, open-ended, and often unexplained that requires that the estranged consciously hold in his or her mind a distressing lack of clarity. Those who suffer must recognize the reality and pain of uncertainty.

But humans hate uncertainty. We have a deep need to know where things stand and what they mean. That makes this first step counterintuitive—and difficult.

Despite and within this ambiguity, those who suffer must find meaning in what seems senseless or meaningless. The pain of estrangement lies in the significance we assign to it, which may or may not be accurate. Far from being a deliberate rejection, a cutoff might be rooted in an estranger's need for distance. Maybe it's a silent plea for change in the dynamics of the relationship. If, for example, you've always bickered when you're together, the estranger could be signaling a wish for more peaceful, tolerant interactions.

Still, living with ambiguous loss is hard. When I was estranged from my only sibling, I was stuck in frozen grief. I felt the estrangement capped my ability to be happy. I struggled with a vortex of questions: *What did I do? Why did this happen? How can I fix it?* Throughout 40 years of separation from my brother, I couldn't find a way to live with the loss—and I never found much peace.

Unique Symptoms of Ambiguous Loss

While the experience of ambiguous loss resembles other kinds of grieving, it's distinguished by key differences. Its hallmarks include:

- Sadness about a situation/event, without knowing why it happened
- Feeling unheard and unsupported
- Feeling others are minimizing your experience
- Thinking you're "being dramatic," "overreacting," or "making a big deal of nothing" (You aren't.)
- Thinking you're going crazy
- Experiencing guilt for feeling so sad, especially if the absent person is still alive
- Vacillating between hope and hopelessness
- Survivor's guilt
- Being consumed by uncertainty

Psychological symptoms can include:

- Anxiety
- Depression
- Obsessive-compulsive disorder

- PTSD
- Drug/alcohol use to numb the pain

How to Cope with Ambiguous Loss

After researching and writing my book, I understood how Pauline Boss's advice could have helped me. Here are her suggestions:

1. Finding Meaning:

- Making sense of the loss through naming it;
- Talking with peers;
- Continuing, but changing family rituals and celebrations.

2. Adjusting Mastery: Modify the natural desire for control and certainty through:

- Acknowledging the world isn't always fair;
- Managing and making decisions;
- Addressing the internal experience through mindfulness exercise, music, etc.

3. Reconstructing Identity: Know who you are now through:

- Finding support from family, friends, or chosen family;
- Redefining your family's boundaries;
- Being flexible as family roles are redefined;
- Identifying who is in/out of the new family system.

4. Normalizing Ambivalence: Manage the anxiety from mixed emotions by:

- Knowing conflicted feelings are normal;
- Discussing them with a professional.

5. Revising Attachment: Let go without certainty of loss through:

- Recognizing that a loved one is both here and gone;
- Grieving what has been lost;
- Acknowledging/celebrating what you still have;
- Finding new human connections.

6. Discovering New Hope: Find hope when your loss remains ambiguous by

- Imagining a new way of being;
- Imagining new future plans or dreams;
- Identifying your spirituality;
- Seeking encouragement through family and friends.

Personally, I did make some progress in accepting estrangement from my brother. Writing 20 minutes a day allowed me to release some of the deep hurts that plagued me. Putting those feelings on the page relieved me of constantly carrying around the pain.

I also learned to recognize that the estrangement wasn't my fault. I stopped personalizing it, realizing that my brother may have had hidden reasons behind cutting me off. (When we reconciled, I learned this was true.)

I also set boundaries with other family members, insisting that they not share information with me about my brother and his family. If I hadn't done this, others could have been pulled into the rift.

If all this seems too daunting, *Stand Alone,* the British organization that serves estranged family members, offers an invaluable list of concrete ways to cope. These include:

- regularly visiting a therapist or counselor who provides a safe space to explore emotions
- practicing meditation to feel more in control of emotions and gain a sense of perspective
- exercising regularly to combat negative feelings associated with estrangement
- leaning on a partner for perspective and support
- accepting feelings as they present themselves.

REFERENCES

Boss, Pauline (1999). *Ambiguous Loss: Learning to Live with Unresolved Grief.* Cambridge, MA: Harvard University Press.

https://www.standalone.org.uk/

What are some of the core beliefs you hold about yourself? (*For example, "I am unlovable" or "I don't deserve to be happy."*) How do your experiences with your siblings in childhood contribute to these beliefs?

How would you describe ambiguous loss? In what ways do you feel you suffer from ambiguous loss due to your sibling estrangement? What tactics have you discovered that help you manage this loss?

_____

_____

_____

_____

_____

_____

_____

_____

_____

_____

_____

_____

_____

_____

Have you been successful in setting boundaries about your estrangement with other family members? What boundaries would you like to set? Come up with a way you can state your needs so that family members will accept your boundary.

Chapter 19
How a Family Cutoff Can Produce Both Grief and Relief

Conflicting emotions mark "ambivalent loss."

KEY POINTS

- The topic of mourning and grief for those who have had a conflicted relationship with a loved one is rarely discussed.
- Ambivalent loss—feelings of grief and relief—come at the end of a relationship when there are unresolved issues, abuse, or bad feelings.
- The estranged feel ambivalent loss because a sibling is no longer in their life, and they realize reconciliation will never happen.

Grief and relief.

These two emotions make a strange pair, yet they're often experienced together by those who have had a conflicted relationship with a loved one.

Ambivalent loss is the deeply confusing state in which grief and relief exist simultaneously. The end of a relationship marked by abuse, unresolved issues, or simply bad feelings frequently provokes ambivalent loss.

An estranged sibling may feel ambivalent loss when a brother or sister is no longer in their life, and they realize reconciliation will never happen. They're relieved the immediate suffering is over—but they're also mourning the hoped-for relationship they must now give up on.

In her bestselling memoir—with the arresting title, *I'm Glad My Mother Died*—Jeannette McCurdy illuminates this rarely discussed phenomenon. McCurdy's heartbreaking book chronicles lifelong abuse inflicted by her narcissistic mother. The Nickelodeon star was pushed into acting at age 6. Her mother mentored her into an eating disorder, controlled every aspect of her life—and then died.

"Her death left me with more questions than answers, more pain than healing, and many layers of grief—the initial grief from her passing, then the grief of accepting her abuse and exploitation of me, and finally, the grief that surfaces now when I miss her and start to cry," McCurdy writes.

Her words succinctly capture the confusion and chaos of ambivalent loss, which produces contradictory feelings of guilt, shame, relief, and longing. Many estranged siblings feel ambivalent loss after making the difficult decision to go "no contact" with a difficult brother or sister.

"I chose to go 'no contact' after I was treated terribly when my parents died a few months ago," a 60-year-old woman wrote in response to a question on my sibling estrangement survey. She had cut off her older brother and sister. "I'm so glad I don't have to deal with the constant drama anymore, but I cry every day because I have no family."

Some feelings of ambivalence are common in any relationship and aren't especially significant, explains London psychotherapist Joshua Miles in an article called, "Understanding ambivalence in loss and grief." (The article appeared on the website for *Counseling Directory*, an organization that promotes talk therapy.) "Few relationships are devoid of or not complicated by some level of hostility or difficulty at some point," Miles writes.

Yet few resources exist addressing mourning and grief for those who have had a conflicted relationship with a loved one. "Where is the book on managing unsaid or unspoken feelings or emotions?" Miles writes. "Where is the book to help guide us through a eulogy or funeral where you wish to speak up, but do not know how due to unspoken ambivalence?"

Different Varieties of grief

To Miles' point, several books discuss other forms of grief, such as:

- **Ambiguous loss:** Psychologist Pauline Boss coined this phrase, describing the experience of losing someone without an event establishing unequivocally that they're gone. Ambiguous loss can occur after a death, miscarriage or divorce or when it's unclear if a relationship is terminated.

- **Complicated grief:** An ongoing, heightened state of mourning that prevents healing may be complicated grief. This condition is characterized by relentless sorrow and rumination over the loss of a loved one.

- **Disenfranchised grief:** Ken Doka, a leading expert on grief counseling and therapy, identified this form of hidden grief. Disenfranchised grief is "a loss that is not or cannot be openly acknowledged, socially sanctioned, or publicly mourned." Examples include infertility the death of an ex-partner, and the death of a pet.

Clearly, these forms of grief may overlap. Ambivalent grief, however, is exceptional: It is characterized by tension, as the individual must manage opposing beliefs, feelings, or behaviors after a loss, whether through estrangement or death.

Why Does Ambivalent Loss Occur?

Several experiences may contribute to ambivalent loss, including:

- **Unfinished or unresolved feelings; lack of contact before a death or a cutoff:** Ambivalent loss may result from a lack of communication, contact, or relationship preceding a death or estrangement. "Grieving can be interrupted when there are unresolved difficulties or feelings towards the person," explains psychotherapist Miles. "When loss is left unexplored, left unspoken or thought about, difficult feelings can surface, leading to ambivalence."

- **An abusive or psychologically damaging relationship:** As McCurdy learned, relief can accompany the passing or cutoff of an abuser. Some may feel guilty that they are relieved by the cutoff or by the death. Reconciling two opposing feelings may give way to shame, as this type of grieving is not socially validated.

- **Remembering the deceased or the estranged differently from others:** Among the complications of ambivalent grief is conflict arising when one person's experience or memory of the estranged or deceased person differs vastly from the perceptions of other family members or friends. A sibling may begin to doubt his or her own negative feelings, resulting in an effort to keep these feelings hidden for fear of upsetting others.

How to Manage Ambivalent Loss

Grief support specialist and therapist Jacque Amweg, who practices in Kansas City, Missouri, offers some recommendations for those faced with ambivalent loss after estrangement or death:

- Put away ideas of what you "should" be feeling. There is no right way to feel or grieve.
- Find someone you can talk to openly and honestly about difficult emotions.
- Take care of "unfinished business" through rituals or activities that promote healing. Journaling and letter-writing may help release some conflicting emotions.
- Keep in mind that relationships are a mixture of good and bad. While grieving, try to remember both.
- Eat well, exercise, and get plenty of rest. Self-care greatly contributes to healing.

Estrangement and death can produce a swirl of conflicting, confusing emotions, as McCurdy writes, that can leave someone with "more questions than answers." In her book, she has taken an enormous step toward healing by publicly acknowledging and accepting her mixed—even contradictory—feelings about her mother.

Although some readers will recoil at her cringe-worthy title, McCurdy's memoir sheds light on the little-discussed but deeply painful experience of ambivalent loss.

REFERENCES

https://www.counselling-directory.org.uk/memberarticles/understanding-ambivalence-in-loss-and-grief

https://www.kchospice.org/grief-difficult/

Describe a time in your life when you experienced "ambivalent loss." What emotions did you encounter? Did the experience leave you "with more questions than answers"? Describe your feelings.

_____

_____

_____

_____

_____

_____

_____

_____

_____

_____

_____

_____

_____

_____

_____

_____

_____

Does your understanding of your sibling deviate significantly from how friends and family perceive your brother or sister? How would you describe your sibling? How would friends and family members describe your sibling?

Have you grieved what you don't have with your sibling? Are you at peace? If not, what do you think you can do to achieve acceptance and balance in your life?

Chapter 20
What Resources Can Help Those Estranged from a Sibling?

There's support for those struggling with a difficult sibling relationship.

KEY POINTS

- Sibling estrangement is a kind of Me-Too movement, as those who suffer are finally breaking silence, rejecting shame, and sharing stories.

- Some researchers say sibling estrangement is epidemic, but it's difficult to accurately measure this stigmatized phenomenon.

- In the last few decades, researchers have begun to conduct studies on the largely unexamined topic of how siblings shape each other's lives.

Sibling estrangement shares some common ground with the "Me-Too" movement. In both, people who have endured a heartbreaking experience are finally breaking silence, rejecting shame, becoming empowered, and finding solidarity in numbers and shared stories.

For more than a century, psychological research has largely ignored the importance of sibling relationships. Sigmund Freud, the founder of psychoanalysis, refers to the sibling relationship just five times in his two dozen volumes of work. Only during the past couple of decades have researchers conducted meaningful studies on how siblings shape one another's lives.

As a consequence, those estranged from their siblings are a large, undisclosed group—one that's not easily measured, in part because people are often reluctant to admit being estranged from a brother or sister. Despite the lack of hard data, some researchers believe that sibling estrangement is grossly underreported and that the phenomenon is epidemic.

Long before I began researching the topic, I noticed the disturbing nature of how others perceive a sibling rupture. "Often, people jump to the conclusion that there must be something wrong with you if you can't get along with your sibling," says Canadian psychotherapist Ali-John Chaudhary, who specializes in sibling relationships and estrangements. "But that's simply not true. Sometimes, there's bad chemistry or dominance/ power struggles or narcissism."

Finding Support

While the British organization, *Stand Alone,* supports people experiencing family estrangement, very few resources are available specifically for siblings. Chaudhary has been a driving force to address this lack of support. He has created several resources:

Sibling estrangement Web site (https://www.siblingestrangement.com): This Web site offers articles, videos, and other resources to help support and empower siblings who are estranged.

Facebook pages: Several private Facebook groups serve those who struggle with sibling relationships—ranging from sibling abuse to narcissistic siblings to estrangement. Some provide a platform to vent and to seek guidance from members who are going through similar experiences. Chaudhary monitors and offers guidance on his page, *Sibling Estrangement—Sharing—Coping—Connecting.* Here, members will find insights and proactive strategies designed to manage difficult sibling situations.

Sibling estrangement support groups on Zoom: Through his Facebook page, Chaudhary offers monthly support groups on Zoom. For a nominal fee, Chaudhary meets with about 10 people from all over the world to discuss their specific challenges resulting from sibling estrangement.

***Brothers, Sisters, Strangers* podcast:** Chaudhary and I have teamed up on a podcast on sibling estrangement that's available on his channel at YouTube.com. Topics range from mourning a sibling relationship to managing destructive rumination to coping with a narcissistic sibling.

Chaudhary, who has struggled in his own relationship with his only sister, says he was motivated to create these resources when he recognized the stunning number of people suffering and the profound nature of their grief.

"This is absolutely a 'Me-Too' movement," he says, "and through these new resources, those of us who are estranged are becoming aware, empowering ourselves, and even redefining the role a sibling plays in our lives."

Why is it important for our society to understand sibling estrangement and offer possibility and comfort to those who suffer from its consequences?

_____

_____

_____

_____

_____

_____

_____

_____

_____

_____

_____

_____

_____

_____

_____

What surprised you in your responses to these journal questions? After answering some of the questions in this journal, can you step back and analyze whether your perceptions about your sibling are accurate or if you are projecting some of your own insecurities on to a brother or sister? What do you know now that you didn't before?

_____

_____

_____

_____

_____

_____

_____

_____

_____

_____

_____

_____

_____

How have you sought support in dealing with sibling estrangement? Could you and your estranged sibling seek therapy to resolve your differences? What are your realistic hopes for your sibling connection?

_____

_____

_____

_____

_____

_____

_____

_____

_____

_____

_____

_____

_____

_____

_____

_____

About the Author

Fern Schumer Chapman is the author of *Brothers, Sisters, Strangers: Sibling Estrangement and the Road to Reconciliation* (Viking/Penguin, 2021). She also writes a blog on sibling estrangement, "Brothers, Sisters, Strangers," for psychologytoday.com, and many of these pieces first appeared on that website. She is a co-host of the *Brothers, Sisters, Strangers* podcast.

Several of her other award-winning books are used in classrooms, including *Is It Night or Day?* and *Like Finding My Twin*. Her memoir, *Motherland* — a Barnes & Noble Discover Great New Writers selection, a finalist for the National Jewish Book Award, and a BookSense76 pick—is a popular choice for book clubs. The Junior Library Guild selected *Stumbling on History* and *Three Stars in the Night Sky* as featured titles.

The Illinois Association of Teachers of English (IATE) named Chapman the "Illinois Author of the Year" in 2004. Twice, Oprah Winfrey shows have featured her books. She lives in northern Illinois and gives dozens of presentations at schools and events each year.

For more information, please visit: www.fernschumerchapman.com